Definitions of Digital Journalism (Studies)

Definitions of Digital Journalism (Studies) offers an authoritative and highly accessible point of entry into current debates and definitions of digital journalism and digital journalism studies.

Journalism continues to evolve as it increasingly shifts to digital forms, practices, and spaces, challenging traditional notions of what journalism is and what it should be. As scholars and practitioners make sense, adapt to, or seek to withstand the different facets of change confronting the field, it is important to clarify the contours of what we are studying. Studies of digital journalism have usually assumed, if not taken for granted, what digital journalism means. But navigating the rapidly expanding scholarship in this area requires clarification of our core concept. This book brings together journalism scholars from around the world to tease out what digital journalism stands for, and what digital journalism scholarship looks like.

This book offers a timely guide for scholars and practitioners of digital journalism. It aims to help undergraduate and graduate students, as well as journalism scholars, in positioning their work within the field of digital journalism studies.

The chapters in this book were originally published as a special issue of the journal *Digital Journalism*.

Scott A. Eldridge II, Assistant Professor, Centre for Media and Journalism Studies, University of Groningen, the Netherlands; Associate Editor, *Digital Journalism*.

Kristy Hess, Associate Professor, Deakin University, Australia; Associate Editor, *Digital Journalism*.

Edson C. Tandoc Jr., Associate Professor, Nanyang Technological University, Singapore; Associate Editor, *Digital Journalism*.

Oscar Westlund, Professor, Oslo Metropolitan University, Norway; research leader for the *Digital Journalism Research Group*; Editor-in-Chief, *Digital Journalism*.

Journalism Studies: Theory and Practice
Series editor: *Bob Franklin, Cardiff School of Journalism, Media and Cultural Studies, Cardiff University, UK*

The journal *Journalism Studies* was established at the turn of the new millennium by Bob Franklin. It was launched in the context of a burgeoning interest in the scholarly study of journalism and an expansive global community of journalism scholars and researchers. The ambition was to provide a forum for the critical discussion and study of journalism as a subject of intellectual inquiry but also an arena of professional practice. Previously, the study of journalism in the UK and much of Europe was a fairly marginal branch of the larger disciplines of media, communication and cultural studies; only a handful of Universities offered degree programmes in the subject. *Journalism Studies* has flourished and succeeded in providing the intended public space for discussion of research on key issues within the field, to the point where in 2007 a sister journal, *Journalism Practice*, was launched to enable an enhanced focus on practice-based issues, as well as foregrounding studies of journalism education, training and professional concerns. Both journals are among the leading ranked journals within the field and publish six issues annually, in electronic and print formats. More recently, 2013 witnessed the launch of a further companion journal *Digital Journalism* to provide a site for scholarly discussion, analysis and responses to the wide ranging implications of digital technologies for the practice and study of journalism. From the outset, the publication of themed issues has been a commitment for all journals. Their purpose is first, to focus on highly significant or neglected areas of the field; second, to facilitate discussion and analysis of important and topical policy issues; and third, to offer readers an especially high quality and closely focused set of essays, analyses and discussions.

The *Journalism Studies: Theory and Practice* book series draws on a wide range of these themed issues from all journals and thereby extends the critical and public forum provided by them. The Editor of the journals works closely with guest editors to ensure that the books achieve relevance for readers and the highest standards of research rigour and academic excellence. The series makes a significant contribution to the field of journalism studies by inviting distinguished scholars, academics and journalism practitioners to discuss and debate the central concerns within the field. It also reaches a wider readership of scholars, students and practitioners across the social sciences, humanities and communication arts, encouraging them to engage critically with, but also to interrogate, the specialist scholarly studies of journalism which this series provides.

Recent titles in the series:

Mapping Citizen and Participatory Journalism in Newsrooms, Classrooms and Beyond
Edited by Melissa Wall

Entrepreneurial Journalism
Edited by Kevin Rafter

Definitions of Digital Journalism (Studies)
Edited by Scott A. Eldridge II, Kristy Hess, Edson C. Tandoc Jr., and Oscar Westlund

For more information about this series, please visit:
www.routledge.com/Journalism-Studies/book-series/JOURNALISM

Definitions of Digital Journalism (Studies)

Edited by
**Scott A. Eldridge II, Kristy Hess,
Edson C. Tandoc Jr., and Oscar Westlund**

 Routledge
Taylor & Francis Group

LONDON AND NEW YORK

First published 2021
by Routledge
2 Park Square, Milton Park, Abingdon, Oxon OX14 4RN

and by Routledge
52 Vanderbilt Avenue, New York, NY 10017

Routledge is an imprint of the Taylor & Francis Group, an informa business

Chapters 1–7 © 2021 Taylor & Francis
Chapter 8 © 2019 Scott A. Eldridge II, Kristy Hess, Edson C. Tandoc, Jr., and
Oscar Westlund. Originally published as Open Access.

British Library Cataloguing in Publication Data
A catalogue record for this book is available from the British Library

ISBN 13: 978-0-367-86007-3

Typeset in Myriad Pro
by Newgen Publishing UK

Publisher's Note
The publisher accepts responsibility for any inconsistencies that may have arisen during
the conversion of this book from journal articles to book chapters, namely the inclusion
of journal terminology.

Disclaimer
Every effort has been made to contact copyright holders for their permission to reprint material
in this book. The publishers would be grateful to hear from any copyright holder who is not here
acknowledged and will undertake to rectify any errors or omissions in future editions of this book.

Contents

Citation Information

The following chapters were originally published in *Digital Journalism*, volume 7, issue 3 (July 2019). When citing this material, please use the original page numbering for each article, as follows:

Chapter 2
What Does Digital Journalism Studies Look Like?
Steen Steensen, Anna M. Grøndahl Larsen, Yngve Benestad Hågvar and Birgitte Kjos Fonn
Digital Journalism, volume 7, issue 3 (July 2019), pp. 320–342

Chapter 3
Why Journalism Is About More Than Digital Technology
Barbie Zelizer
Digital Journalism, volume 7, issue 3 (July 2019), pp. 343–350

Chapter 4
The 5Ws and 1H of Digital Journalism
Silvio Waisbord
Digital Journalism, volume 7, issue 3 (July 2019), pp. 351–358

Chapter 5
Digital Journalism as Symptom, Response, and Agent of Change in the Platformed Media Environment
Jean Burgess and Edward Hurcombe
Digital Journalism, volume 7, issue 3 (July 2019) pp. 359–367

Chapter 6
Locating the "Digital" in Digital Journalism Studies: Transformations in Research
Sue Robinson, Seth C. Lewis and Matt Carlson
Digital Journalism, volume 7, issue 3 (July 2019), pp. 368–377

Chapter 7
Digital Journalism: Defined, Refined, or Re-defined
Andrew Duffy and Peng Hwa Ang
Digital Journalism, volume 7, issue 3 (July 2019), pp. 378–385

Chapter 8

Navigating the Scholarly Terrain: Introducing the Digital Journalism Studies Compass
Scott A. Eldridge II, Kristy Hess, Edson C. Tandoc, Jr. and Oscar Westlund
Digital Journalism, volume 7, issue 3 (July 2019), pp. 386–403

For any permission-related enquiries please visit:
www.tandfonline.com/page/help/permissions

Notes on Contributors

Yngve Benestad Hågvar, Department of Journalism and Media Studies, Oslo Metropolitan University, Norway.

Jean Burgess, Digital Media Research Centre, Queensland University of Technology, Brisbane, QLD, Australia.

Matt Carlson, Hubbard School of Journalism and Mass Communication, University of Minnesota, Minneapolis, MN, USA.

Andrew Duffy, Wee Kim Wee School of Communication and Information, Nanyang Technological University, Jurong West, Singapore.

Scott A. Eldridge II, Centre for Media and Journalism Studies, University of Groningen, the Netherlands.

Anna M. Grøndahl Larsen, Department of Media and Communication, University of Oslo, Norway.

Kristy Hess, School of Communication and Creative Arts, Deakin University, Burwood, NSW, Australia.

Edward Hurcombe, Digital Media Research Centre, Queensland University of Technology, Brisbane, QLD, Australia.

Peng Hwa Ang, Wee Kim Wee School of Communication and Information, Nanyang Technological University, Jurong West, Singapore.

Birgitte Kjos Fonn, Department of Journalism and Media Studies, Oslo Metropolitan University, Norway.

Seth C. Lewis, School of Journalism and Communication, University of Oregon, Eugene, OR, USA.

Sue Robinson, School of Journalism and Mass Communication, University of Wisconsin-Madison, Madison, WI, USA.

Steen Steensen, Department of Journalism and Media Studies, Oslo Metropolitan University, Norway.

Edson C. Tandoc Jr., Wee Kim Wee School of Communication and Information, Nanyang Technological University, Nanyang, Singapore.

Silvio Waisbord, School of Media and Public Affairs, George Washington University, Washington, DC, USA.

Oscar Westlund, Department of Journalism and Media Studies, Oslo Metropolitan University, Norway.

Barbie Zelizer, Annenberg School for Communication, University of Pennsylvania, Philadelphia, PA, USA.

Digital Journalism (Studies): Defining the Field

Scott A. Eldridge II, Kristy Hess, Edson C. Tandoc Jr., and Oscar Westlund

Introduction

This book brings together a collection of articles published in a *Digital Journalism* special issue in 2019 titled "Digital Journalism (Studies) – Defining the Field", edited by the four of us in our capacity as the *Digital Journalism* editorial team. We had three ambitions with this special issue (c.f. Eldridge, Hess, Tandoc & Westlund, 2019). First, to offer a review of research that has been published in this journal since its launch in 2013 to examine the current state of play. We commissioned a review article by a team of scholars with expertise in such reviews (Steensen, Larsen, Hågvar & Fonn, 2019). Second, we wanted to launch a new article format for the journal – the invited conceptual article (Westlund, 2018) – and commissioned five articles to conceptualise "digital journalism" from different research foci (Burgess & Hurcombe, 2019; Duffy & Peng Hwa, 2019; Robinson, Lewis & Carlson, 2019; Waisbord, 2019; Zelizer, 2019). Third, building on these articles, we authored an analysis of the breadth of discussions which have shaped the field of Digital Journalism Studies, outlined our vision of this field, and established the editorial agenda of *Digital Journalism* going forward, guided by the Digital Journalism Studies Compass we introduced. In line with our vision for the journal and the rigorous work being developed in the field, all articles in this special issue were rigorously peer-reviewed by experts in the field. This book republishes the articles from the special issue in the original order and shape.

At the heart of the special issue and republished in this book, the five conceptual articles provide useful points of entry to "digital journalism", something which many scholars have referred to in their work and discussed among colleagues. Yet, often this has occurred without first establishing a shared understanding of what "digital journalism" is. The conceptual articles serve as points of entry for addressing this shortcoming in our discussion of digital journalism. By providing conceptual anchor points, these essays offer points of reflection which can be incorporated both in future research projects and journalistic practice. For the journal, this collection of conceptual articles has offered inspiration for other scholars working to advance the field of Digital Journalism Studies, including in a widening range of conceptual articles. Throughout 2019 and spring 2020, *Digital Journalism* published more conceptual articles focusing on *Alternative News Media* (Holt, Figenschou & Frischlich, 2019), *API-based Research* (Venturini & Rogers, 2019), *Creativity* (Witschge, Deuze & Willemsen, 2019), *Attention* (Myllylahti, 2019), *Placeification* (Gutsche, Jr. & Hess, 2020), *Meso News-Space* (Tenenboim & Kligler-Vilenchik, 2020) and *Confirmation Bias* (Ling, 2020). Each of these offers a clear conceptual definition of a key idea for Digital Journalism

Studies, while also including a discussion of implications for future research and benefit to empirical research.

Since its release, the special issue, which this book re-establishes, has gained traction in the field; each of the conceptual essays, the review article, and our analysis has garnered thousands of downloads, are regularly cited in other scholarly works, and have been recognised by the authors' peers, receiving multiple nominations for annual awards. We are immensely grateful to the contributors for rising to this challenge and producing highly reflective and clarifying articles.

We are excited about the opportunity to bring this collection of fine articles into this collected volume with Routledge. This introduction now turns toward outlining the academic discussions which have shaped the field, and the contributions made first in the special issue of *Digital Journalism* mapping the field, and now collected in this volume.

Digital Journalism: Past, Present, Future

The book continues in Chapter 2 with the lead research article from the special issue, in which Steensen and colleagues reviewed research publications in *Digital Journalism*, prominent book publications in the field, and the impact of this research. Steensen et al. analysed keywords and citations across all issues of *Digital Journalism* to identify the dominant themes, degrees of diversity and interdisciplinarity, as well as biases and blind spots. They conclude by offering an initial and empirically based definition reflective of this body of work, from which they problematise research developments. For example, they argue that some concepts which have been introduced in publications are then rarely used by others. They also identify a tendency to ignore (often unintentionally) existing developments and concepts in the field while building new ways of seeing digital journalism. A more delicate approach to stitching the new with the existing is needed to balance continuity and change.

Next, Zelizer offers a provocation in Chapter 3 "Why Journalism Is About More Than Digital Technology". To Zelizer, the digital is not an environment; it is a modality, a stage on which journalism plays out. She argues we would be best served to assess not only what is changing, but what structures and practices, ideas, and values continue to stay the same. In other words, how much does a term like digital necessitate a nod to technology? What are the foundations that sustain and shape the very notion of "journalism"? Zelizer argues that digital journalism takes its meaning from both practice and rhetoric. Its practice as newsmaking embodies a set of expectations, specific practices, capabilities, and limitations relative to those associated with pre-digital and non-digital forms, reflecting a difference of degree rather than kind. Its rhetoric heralds the hopes and anxieties associated with sustaining the journalistic enterprise as worthwhile. Digital journalism, she contends, constitutes the most recent of many conduits over time that have allowed us to imagine optimal links between journalism and the public. Zelizer argues that the rise of networks, de-institutionalisation and de-professionalisation, increased participation, and personal agency have all been viewed as positive for enhancing democracy, but we should always consider whether some structures – hierarchical, institutional, or professional – might indeed be a good thing. She also calls for broadened discussion on transparency, from anonymity in the news to the issues present in the blurring of boundaries between fantasy and reality. Zelizer asks us to take more time to consider how news is produced and avoid what has been described elsewhere in academic literature as "digital distraction". Ultimately, she implores scholars to give a greater nod to history rather than a fixation on novelty, something Baym (2018) has argued elsewhere in her analysis of the music industries, and Hamilton (2018) has made in a push for examining the origins of broadcasting.

In Chapter 4, Waisbord repurposes the classic "5Ws and 1H" framework for understanding digital journalism. A brief detour into the history of this time-honoured formula is perhaps pertinent to consider the balance of change and continuity that we will emphasise later in this chapter. The idea of the "5Ws and 1H", for example, stretches back as far as Aristotle and was popularised in poetry by British writer Rudyard Kipling at the turn of the 20th century. It emerged as a result of significant social and technological change and signalled a shift from stories written with a more flamboyant narrative style (see e.g. Errico, 1997). It reminds us how industrialisation and technology can unsettle journalism practice but that some traditional values and approaches can also be re-invigorated or reinvented over time.

Waisbord salvages the "crumbling" pyramid model of news as an analytical device to assess the unprecedented developments in journalism. He highlights some of the obvious stakeholders and practices under this framework: *who* – anyone who uses the internet; *what* – content of digital journalism can be anything; *when* – shattered modern notions of time in news production and consumption; *where* – elides barriers such as geography and language to reach audiences; and *how* – the changing, at times disappearing, well-defined and agreed-upon norms and conventions shaping journalism practice.

However, it is his discussion around the *why* that offers especially profound insight for digital journalism scholarship. Here Waisbord argues the very purpose of journalism now features such a chaotic array of motivations – from issues of self-presentation to social connection and support "along with the mainstays of making money, to scrutinise and reinforce power, educate, and influence" – that all must be carefully considered in an environment now designed for journalism to be practised at a constant hyper-speed. Further, in his view, the expanding networked settings and practices of journalism require deeper consideration as the networks of digital journalism are now "far more complex, open, noisy, and unruly". He draws on Peters and Witschge (2015) to suggest that while "participation in news" may not necessarily have virtuous democratic consequences, there are certainly more news producers that highlight the growing power of platforms such as Facebook and Google. Waisbord also points to the importance of scholars paying greater attention to what is socially considered and used as news.

In Chapter 5, Burgess and Hurcombe draw on their expertise in digital media studies to provide an interdisciplinary perspective on digital journalism. They prefer to focus on the importance of the social as reference to the rise of social media or news platforms that are "born digital". They extend the concept of social news to consider the rise of sites such as BuzzFeed, Junkee and PedestrianTV, which often promote politically progressive causes in their coverage and are directly distinguishable in the vernacular conventions and pop-culture sensibilities of social media. Burgess and Hurcombe emphasise the new genres and modes of journalistic storytelling that exploit connected digital technologies, highlighting the changing role of Twitter for "social listening", and as a tool to gather news tip-offs or source quotes for stories. They draw attention to the increasing power of packaged metrics (based on social media data) that now contribute to shaping journalistic practices, values, and priorities. This leaves media institutions increasingly responsive to these metrics and hence "mirroring the priorities and values of the platforms themselves" or what Caplan and boyd (2018) refer to as "institutional isomorphism". Such an approach like "social news" must always be careful not to subsume or overlook journalism's relationship to broader social realms and social connections beyond digital processes, but the "transformative and isomorphic" impacts of these new platforms and practices are certainly worthy of our attention.

Next, in Chapter 6, Robinson, Lewis, and Carlson not only adopt a phrase like transformation to discuss digital journalism; they set out to develop a theoretical framework with which to understand this process. They offer a distinct contrast to Waisbord's emphasis on the *revolutionary* changes in social and public life. To Robinson, Lewis and Carlson, transformation is a richer idea than that of change or revolution because it does not assume or equate to progress or the shedding of endemic structures. Rather, it encourages a research perspective "centered on change whilst also allowing for maintenance of a foundational status quo". Zelizer also issues caution over reference to "revolution" in Digital Journalism Studies given that "most enduring change unfolds in bits and pieces, with no technology ever staying the same for long". Robinson and colleagues suggest that *transformation* offers a way forward for Digital Journalism Studies to encompass how the news media ecology is being reconstituted by mobile technology, social media, and other digital platforms. The process, or myriad practices, that shape transformation can be factored in six commitments – context sensitivity, holistic relationality, comparative inclination, normative awareness, embedded communicative power, and methodological plurality. In other words, transformation becomes a framework with which to understand the balance between continuity and change. Robinson, Lewis, and Carlson position digital journalism as a subfield of journalism studies, providing a handle for us to problematise how to situate digital journalism scholarship, which we shall discuss shortly. Their approach to transformation certainly complements those taken by others in this volume.

Duffy and Ang highlight in Chapter 7 – joining the efforts of all of our authors in this volume – the difficulty in disentangling journalism from digital technology. In an approach similar to Steensen and colleagues' work, they draw on keywords from articles in *Digital Journalism* to reveal a persistent newsroom-first approach (an argument made in earlier contexts by Wahl-Jorgensen, 2009) that tends to emphasise how digitisation brings opportunities to journalism that have not been realised or explore a recurring theme of boundary work. Instead, they suggest that Digital Journalism Studies should lose the normative accretions surrounding journalism and begin with the principles of digitisation. They balance a more direct, yet broader, societal approach to calling for scholarship that privileges the "digital" over "journalism". As a result, digital journalism becomes the embodiment of digital principles: "Digitisation sets the agenda for journalism to follow, rather than journalism setting the agenda for its digital incarnation to live up to – or not". By digitisation, they draw on the scholarship of Brennen and Kreiss (2016) to refer to the way domains of social life are restructured around digital communication and media infrastructures. A shift in this direction, they suggest, requires a greater distance from legacy news production and the newsroom to explore how digitisation is a feature of society and how journalism articulates or informs this.

Altogether, these conceptual articles crystallise the different perspectives and approaches to digital journalism that – when read as a collection – reveal the synergies, provocations, and clear epistemological differences influencing research in this space.

The final chapter advances these ideas by refining and defining Digital Journalism Studies. The editorial team (Eldridge, Hess, Tandoc, and Westlund) offer an analysis of the emergent body of work defining this academic field, offering a guiding narrative for a field of Digital Journalism Studies to attune its work to. In doing so, we hope to offer some clarity for researchers in the field, while embracing the diversity of ideas and ways of connecting the digital with journalism. The central concern is to lay the foundations for digital journalism as existing within its own distinctive field, moving beyond its place as a subfield of journalism studies. The article outlines the "Digital Journalism Studies Compass" (DJSC) to provide clarity as scholars navigate and plot the directions that Digital Journalism Studies may take in the future. By arguing for approaches that embrace the digital coupled with journalism, and continuity alongside change, we offer a heuristic tool that scholars and students can employ as they navigate the digital journalism space as part of their own scholarly pursuits, enriching discussions in this exciting scholarly terrain.

We see this book as an opportunity to collect by tapping into contemporary debates and research in digital journalism, seeing this volume as a point of departure for developing research projects. In doing so, we see this book as complementing a series of recent handbooks which have helped scholars introduce digital aspects of journalism and journalism studies (Wahl-Jorgensen & Hanitzsch, 2020) and further establish a field of Digital Journalism Studies which endeavours to make sense of the specific developments of digital journalism research in its own right (Eldridge & Franklin, 2019). As a snapshot of this burgeoning field, these volumes and others (e.g. Franklin & Canter, 2019; Witschge et al. 2016) reflect the intellectual depths being plumbed by scholars working in this field.

References

Baym, Nancy (2018) *Playing to the Crowd: Musicians, Audiences and the Intimate Work of Connection*. New York: New York University Press.

Brennen, J. Scott and Kreiss, Daniel (2016) Digitalization. In Klaus Bruhn Jensen and Robert Craig (Eds), *The International Encyclopedia of Communication Theory and Philosophy*. Hoboken, NJ: Wiley Online Library. https://doi:10.1002/9781118766804.wbiect111

Burgess, Jean and Hurcombe, Edward (2019) Digital journalism as symptom, response, and agent of change, *Digital Journalism*, 7(3): 359–367.

Caplan, Robyn and boyd, danah (2018) Isomorphism through algorithms: Institutional dependencies in the case of Facebook, *Big Data & Society*, https://doi.org/10.1177/2053951718757253

Duffy, Andrew and Peng Hwa, Ang (2019) Digital Journalism: Defined, refined, or re-defined, *Digital Journalism*, 7(3): 378–385.

Eldridge, Scott and Franklin, Bob (2019) *The Routledge Handbook of Developments in Digital Journalism Studies*. London: Routledge.

Eldridge, Scott, Hess, Kristy, Tandoc, Edson and Westlund, Oscar (2019) Navigating the scholarly terrain: Introducing the Digital Journalism compass, *Digital Journalism*, 7(3): 386–403.

Errico, Marcus (1997) The evolution of the summary news lead, *Media History Monographs*, 1(1), np.

Franklin, Bob and Canter, Lily (2019) *Digital Journalism Studies: The Key Concepts*. London: Routledge.

Gutsche, Jr., Robert E. and Hess, Kristy (2020) Placeification: The transformation of digital news spaces into "places" of meaning, *Digital Journalism*, https://doi:10.1080/21670811.2020.1737557

Hamilton, James (2018) Excavating concepts of broadcasting: Developing a method of cultural research using digitised historical periodicals, *Digital Journalism*, 6(9):1136–1149

Holt, Kristoffer, Figenschou, Tine Ustad and Lena Frischlich (2019) Key dimensions of alternative news media, *Digital Journalism*, 7(7): 860–869, https://doi:10.1080/21670811.2019.1625715

Ling, Richard (2020) Confirmation bias in the era of mobile news consumption: The social and psychological dimensions, *Digital Journalism*. https://doi:10.1080/21670811.2020.1766987

Myllylahti, Merja (2019) Paying attention to attention: A conceptual framework for studying news reader revenue models related to platforms, *Digital Journalism*, https://doi:10.1080/21670811.2019.1691926

Peters, Chris and Witschge, Tamara (2015) From grand narratives of democracy to small expectations of participation: Audiences, citizenship, and interactive tools in digital journalism, *Journalism Practice*, 9(1), 19–34.

Robinson, Sue, Lewis, Seth C. and Carlson, Matt (2019) Locating the 'digital' in Journalism Studies: Transformations in research, *Digital Journalism*, 7(3): 368–377.

Steensen Steen, Larsen, Anna M., Hågvar, Yngve and Fonn, Birgitte (2019) What does Digital Journalism Studies look like?, *Digital Journalism*, 7(3): 320–342.

Tenenboim, Ori and Kligler-Vilenchik, Neta (2020) The meso news-space: Engaging with the news between the public and private domains, *Digital Journalism*, https://doi:10.1080/21670811.2020.1745657

Venturini, Tommaso and Rogers, Richard (2019) "API-based research" or how can digital sociology and Journalism Studies learn from the Facebook and Cambridge Analytica data breach, *Digital Journalism*, 7(4), 532–540, https://doi:10.1080/21670811.2019.1591927

Wahl-Jorgensen, Karin (2009) On the newsroom-centricity of journalism ethnography. In S. Elizabeth Bird (Ed.), *Journalism and Anthropology* (pp. 21–35). Bloomington, IN: Indiana University Press.

Wahl-Jorgensen, Karin and Hanitzsch, Thomas (2020) *The Handbook of Journalism Studies*. London: Routledge.

Waisbord, Silvio (2019) The 5Ws and 1H of digital journalism, *Digital Journalism*, 7(3): 351–358.

Westlund, Oscar (2018) Editorial, *Digital Journalism*, 6(10), 1288–1293.

Witschge, Tamara, Anderson, C. W., Domingo, David and Hermida, Alfred (2016) *The SAGE Handbook of Digital Journalism*. London: SAGE.

Witschge, Tamara, Deuze, Mark and Willemsen, Sofie (2019) Creativity in (Digital) Journalism Studies: Broadening our perspective on journalism practice, *Digital Journalism*, 7(7): 972–979.

Zelizer, Barbie (2019) Why journalism is about more than digital technology, *Digital Journalism*, 7(3): 343–350.

What Does Digital Journalism Studies Look Like?

Steen Steensen, Anna M. Grøndahl Larsen, Yngve Benestad Hågvar and Birgitte Kjos Fonn

ABSTRACT

This article analyses the characteristics of digital journalism studies through an empirical investigation of all articles published in the journal *Digital Journalism*, from its launch in 2013 to issue 6, 2018. The aim of the analysis is to identify dominant themes and degrees of diversity and interdisciplinary in digital journalism studies, and to identify biases and blind spots. The article is based on analysis of keywords, abstracts and references used in all articles published in the journal. The findings suggest that while the research published in *Digital Journalism* is firmly situated within journalism studies, it has a stronger emphasis on technology, platforms, audience and the present. The article also finds that digital journalism studies, as seen in *Digital Journalism*, is dominated by perspectives from the social sciences, while largely ignoring digital journalism as a meaning-making system, and that the field of research could benefit from the application of theories and perspectives from the humanities and to some extent from theoretical computer science and informatics. Finally, the article argues that digital journalism studies suffers from a lack of connections between empirical research and the many conceptual discussions that dominate the (sub)field.

Introduction

In his editorial for the inaugural issue of the journal *Digital Journalism* in 2013, Franklin argued that the absence of a journal devoted to the changes to journalism and society brought forth by digital technologies had "constituted an extraordinary omission in scholarly publishing provision within the field of journalism studies" (2013, 1). The aim of the new journal was to fill that void by becoming "a repository for research-based studies which catalogue these changes" (2013, 2). In other words: *Digital Journalism* wanted to become a hub for the study of digital journalism and an archive of its development.

During the six years that have passed since the launch of the journal, it has undoubtedly made its mark not only as a hub for a (sub)field within journalism studies but also within the broader discipline of communication. According to the Google Scholar journal ranking, which masseurs a journal's impact over the past five years (the h5 index), *Digital Journalism* became the fourth most influential journal within the discipline of communication during 2018.[1] The journal thereby surpassed all the other major journalism journals (*Journalism Studies, Journalism: Theory, Practice & Criticism, Journalism Practice*, and *Journalism & Mass Communication Quarterly*). Although citation metrics do not tell the whole story of a journal's impact and significance, it is remarkable that a journal established to cover a sub-field may in fact outgrow the field it is supposed to be subordinate to.

It is therefore time to stop and reflect over what digital journalism studies has become. Does the success of the journal *Digital Journalism* imply that digital journalism studies has become a scholarly field of its own? If so; what are the relationship between digital journalism studies and journalism studies, the field it was established as subordinated to? This article takes those questions as its starting point in an attempt at answering the question posed in the title: What does digital journalism studies look like?

There has been no lack of attempts at defining digital journalism studies in recent years. Several conceptual books and journal articles—most notably the two handbooks edited by Witschge et al. (2016b) and Franklin and Eldridge II (2017)—have contributed extensively to the scholarly discussion on what digital journalism studies is and how it develops. However, not many have taken an empirical approach beyond the review of literature in search for answers. Our contribution is an empirical one. We will present and discuss an extensive empirical analysis of all articles published in *Digital Journalism*, the journal, which the founding editor Franklin, as cited above, wanted to become the repository of digital journalism studies. Before we present exactly what and how we have conducted this empirical analysis, we will present some of the ideas discussed in the literature. After all, there is more to digital journalism studies than what can be found in the journal *Digital Journalism*.

The Rise of Digital Journalism Studies

The phrase "digital journalism" first appeared in scholarly publications like *Newspaper Research Journal* and reports from the Nieman lab at Harvard around the time the Internet became publicly available through the World Wide Web during the mid-1990s. Some of these early publications point to future directions and discussions of great significance, like Harper (1996), who investigated to what degree US newspaper editors were concerned with making a revenue with the online editions they were planning to launch. The study of digital journalism was, in other words, from the very beginning enmeshed in an economic discourse, in which how to finance journalism in a digital age has been one of the core questions. Furthermore, Fulton et al. (1994) discussed what journalism is and who is a journalist in a digital age when "everyone can report and edit the news". Fundamental questions of who and what journalism is and can be in a digital age has in other words also dominated the scholarship on digital journalism from the very beginning.

However, "digital journalism" did not become a common phrase in academic publications before much later. The phrase occurs in 34 different publications between 1995 and 2000, rising to 168 publications between 2000 and 2005, according to a

Google Scholar search. Scholars were more occupied with analyzing "online", "web" or "multimedia" journalism during these years. Between 2005 and 2010, Google Scholar returns 796 hits on the phrase, rising to 3790 between 2010 and 2015, and 6820 from 2015 to 2018. Such search results must of course be corrected with the general increase in all kinds of publications available through Google Scholar searches during the same years. Nevertheless, the study of "digital journalism" is predominantly a post-2010 phenomenon, and there is probably no coincidence that the massive increase in scholarly attention to the phrase coincides with the launch of *Digital Journalism* in 2013.

Influences from STS

The shift of attention from "online", "web", "multimedia", etc., to "digital" in scholarly publications might seem insignificant, but represents a discursive change from talking about the various technological aspects of journalism in a digital age to talking about "the whole world of cultural, economic, social, and technological aspects of the contemporary field of journalism" (Witschge et al. 2016a, 2). This discursive shift also implies a non-deterministic turn away from looking at how digital technology affects journalism, to how journalism, in conjunction with other social institutions, is both shaped by and shapes what a digital society is and how it develops. Such a turn is heavily influenced by science and technology studies (STS) and theories that emphasize how technology is socially constructed (Bijker, Hughes, and Pinch 1987; Bijker 2009).

Boczkowski's (2004) book *Digitizing the News* represents a seminal source of influence for this discursive change as it introduced STS perspectives to journalism studies and emphasized the mutual shaping of journalism and technology through ethnographic research in newsrooms. The book spurred a strand of ethnographic research within journalism studies that empirically investigated the connections between, and codependency and mutual shaping of, journalism and technology (see for instance the two edited volumes Domingo and Paterson 2011; Paterson and Domingo 2008). This, in turn, inspired the methodological application of sociotechnical theories like actor-network theory (ANT) in digital journalism studies, which emphasize not only the mutual shaping of journalism and technology but also juxtapose human, technological and material actors and actants as equally important to this mutual shaping. Such approaches have been praised for their non-deterministic, unbiased and empirical orientation (Turner 2005; Primo and Zago 2015), but also critiqued for their inclination to produce nothing more than dull descriptions (Benson 2017).

Nevertheless, STS approaches have contributed valuable nuances to the relationship between journalism and technology—approaches, which undoubtedly have shaped how the "digital" is understood in digital journalism studies as something, which goes beyond binary code to include social, political, cultural, epistemological and economic discourses. However, given the emphasis on "digital" and thereby technology in digital journalism studies, one could perhaps anticipate that theories and disciplinary perspective from academic fields like computer science, informatics and information science also would influence the scholarly work at great length. This is something we will empirically investigate in this article as part of our first research question:

RQ1: What are the dominant themes and disciplinary perspectives in the journal *Digital Journalism*?

The Multidisciplinarity of (Digital) Journalism Studies

RQ1 presupposes that digital journalism studies, as it is presented in *Digital Journalism*, is dominated by more than one disciplinary perspective, just like journalism studies is. *Journalism Studies* is a field traditionally marked by approaches and perspectives from sociology, political science, cultural studies, language studies and history (Zelizer 2004). In a longitudinal analysis of disciplinary perspectives in the journals *Journalism Studies* and *Journalism—Theory, Practice & Criticism*, Steensen and Ahva (2015) found that sociology was the main source of influence in journalism studies and that this discipline had become increasingly dominant. Political science perspectives, which dominated the field in the early 2000s, was the second most common discipline, while cultural studies, language studies and history played minor parts. In addition, fields and disciplines like business and administration, economics, law and philosophy were also present, while technological perspectives were on the rise.

The question is if digital journalism studies is marked by the same disciplinary patterns as journalism studies, or if this (sub)field has different sources of influence. The academic metadiscourse on digital journalism studies (i.e., scholarly publications discussing what digital journalism studies is) suggests that the field is marked by a fixation with the blurring of boundaries that allegedly used to be clear cut. Examples include boundaries between journalists and audiences, professionals and amateurs, organizations and individuals, marketing and news, automation and manual labor, tech developers and journalists, different kinds of modality (text, video, audio, etc.), facts and opinion, objectivity and subjectivity, real and fake news, distributors and producers, technologies and content, consumption and production, and the private and the public. In the words of Eldridge II and Franklin (2017, 4) digital journalism studies "can be understood through the ways it has embraced unclear definitional boundaries around journalism as it has experienced radical change in the past few decades". The (sub)field is in other words dominated by a discourse of change, expressed for instance as a "need to address changing contexts and new practices, need to reconsider theories and develop research strategies" (Witschge et al. 2016a, 2). This discourse of change has, according to Ahva and Steensen (2017), evolved from viewing change as a revolution to change as deconstruction, in the sense that digital journalism studies today is preoccupied with deconstructing previously established notions of what journalism is. In this article, we will investigate the degrees to which this emphasis on change creates new and different interdisciplinary paths for digital journalism studies as we seek answers to the following research question:

RQ2: To what extent and in what ways are articles in *Digital Journalism* cross- and interdisciplinary?

The emphasis on change and deconstruction in the metadiscourse of digital journalism studies should imply that digital journalism studies reaches beyond the disciplinary paths established by journalism studies in search for new ways of conceptualizing and analyzing its objects of study. In other words: One could reasonably expect digital journalism studies to be both highly cross-disciplinary, implying that its developments are understood from a variety of disciplinary points of view, and highly interdisciplinary, implying that the various disciplinary perspectives are brought together to create new conceptual frameworks that make sense of it all.

However, when researchers put much emphasis on the things that changes, there is always the risk that the things that do not change are neglected and that descriptions of change become more important than figuring out the deeper relations between journalism and society. In the words of Peters and Carlson (2018, 3); "one of the dangers in placing change above solidity is the increased difficulty of moving from the surface to engage in deeper social questions". It is therefore necessary to ask if digital journalism studies, as it is presented in *Digital Journalism*, is characterized by any such shortcomings. Boczkowski and Mitchelstein (2017) have already argued that digital journalism studies is marked by two limitations: (1) the ability to connect empirical findings from digital journalism studies across other domains of digital culture and (2) a lack of conceptual exchanges with other fields and disciplines. Our third and last research question embarks from such arguments as we assume that digital journalism studies might have some biases and blind spots, which could be detected through empirical investigations:

> RQ3: What, if any, are the empirical and theoretical biases and blind spots of research published in the journal *Digital Journalism*?

Methodology

We will answer the three research questions through an analysis of keywords, abstracts and references of articles published in *Digital Journalism*. This design allows us to do an analysis of *all* articles published in the one journal that has risen to become the most central to the (sub)field of digital journalism studies. Moreover, the research design allows us to compare the findings with a similar analysis of articles in the journals *Journalism Studies and Journalism: Theory, Practice and Criticism* (Steensen and Ahva 2015).

However, the approach has some limitations, as digital journalism scholarship is also published in other journals, and in reports and books. An analysis of the journal *Digital Journalism* can therefore only to a certain extent paint a picture of the status of the (sub)field of digital journalism studies. Moreover, analyzing keywords, abstracts and references does not give a full account of the research published since we have not included analysis of full articles. To overcome this weakness, we have combined qualitative and quantitative, and inductive and deductive research approaches, to secure that our findings are as reliable as possible. We will present and discuss these methodological procedures below, but first we will make transparent how we obtained the data.

We downloaded the metadata for all articles published in *Digital Journalism* from issue 1, 2013 to issue 6, 2018 from the journal's homepage by using the reference manager software Zotero.[2] The analysis followed the methodological procedure developed by Steensen and Ahva (2015), with some additional analytical steps. Since an article's references are not part of the metadata that can be downloaded with the use of a reference manager software like Zotero, we had to obtain the references from the Web of Science (WoS) database. Unfortunately, the WoS database had only stored metadata (including references) from *Digital Journalism* from the 2015 volume and onwards, so we were not able to get the references from articles published in the two first volumes. The data obtained from the journal's home page and from the WoS database was imported to Excel for analysis.

Keywords

Keywords are words and phrases authors select to categorize their work. However, there are no standardized ways of writing keywords and journals normally provide few guidelines. According to *Digital Journalism's* style guide, authors must provide between 6 and 8 keywords. The publisher, Taylor & Francis, offers some advice on how to write keywords in their online author service section. These advices include search optimization and relevance to the focus of the work presented (Taylor & Francis 2015). We therefore assume that authors choose keywords that provide an as accurate and search friendly depiction of their work as possible, implying that topics covered and theories and methods used are likely to appear as keywords. We therefore believe that analyzing keywords is a fruitful way of detecting dominant themes in articles across a journal.

We extracted all keywords from all articles (1740 keywords from 295 articles) and first identified all the unique keywords in the material. This involved not only removing keywords that were repeated in several articles, but also grouping keywords together that perhaps were spelled differently but in essence were the same. Examples here include keywords like "journalist" and "journalists", which we grouped together as the same keyword, as we did with keywords like "Actor-Network Theory", "Actor Network Theory" and "ANT".

This initial structuring of keywords made it possible to identify 935 unique keywords used in the 295 articles. We then added an additional layer of synchronization and grouped keywords that in essence pointed to the same thing into one clustered keyword. An example here is keywords like "Facebook", "Twitter" and "social media" which we grouped together as the clustered keyword "social media". This process gave us 506 unique and clustered keywords, which we then analyzed to see if we could detect any common themes. Through a hermeneutic process of coding and recoding the clustered keywords according to themes, we were able to identify several thematic clusters of keywords.

Abstracts

The analysis of keywords provides a broad overview of the topics covered in *Digital Journalism*. However, analyzing keywords has some weaknesses. We can for instance not take for granted that theoretical and disciplinary perspectives are visible as keywords. To further investigate the interdisciplinary character of *Digital Journalism* as well as the dominant disciplinary perspectives and theories, we carried out an analysis of abstracts. Abstracts should be compelling short summaries of articles, including research questions and main findings (Taylor & Francis 2015). Thus, while abstracts do not give a full picture of articles, they will probably indicate the disciplinary, theoretical and empirical emphasis of articles.

First, we analyzed abstracts deductively according to main disciplinary categories. The disciplinary categories were pre-defined, based on Zelizer's (2004) discussion of the interdisciplinarity of journalism studies and Steensen and Ahva's (2015) similar analysis of abstracts in *Journalism Studies* and *Journalism: Theory, Practice & Criticism*. The categories included political science, sociology, language, philosophy, history, business and administration, technology and law. This first part of the abstract analysis can be characterized as qualitative content analysis, in which the aim is to identify latent content, implying "a research technique for making replicable and valid inferences from texts (or other meaningful matter) to the contexts of their use" (Krippendorff 2004, 18).

The deductive analysis of abstracts was done in two steps: first, we read and analyzed half of the abstracts (140, sorting the abstracts chronologically on publication year, every other abstract was read and analyzed), and categorized each abstract according to dominant disciplinary perspectives, and which theories (if any) were mentioned. Many abstracts included more than one disciplinary perspective and the categorizing of disciplinary perspective was highly interpretive. In order to secure the quality of this analysis, the authors read the material several times and re-categorized some of the material based on discussions among the authors. Given the degree of interpretation and the relatively small *n*, we will not present the findings in specific numbers, but rather use broader categories like "majority", "minority", "about one third", etc. Finally, we mapped the presence of specific theories in abstracts. For this reading, we did not predefine any categories, as we wanted to map all theories mentioned. For each abstract, we asked whether the abstract included explicit mention of theoretical perspectives (categorized "yes"/"no") or not. In addition, we wrote down which theoretical theories that were explicitly mentioned.

Second, and in addition to the deductive analysis of abstracts described above, we performed an inductive analysis of abstracts. Here, authors conducted a qualitative close reading of 95 abstracts from articles in issue 1 and 3 in all volumes. The purpose of this reading was to add nuance to the findings, and capture potential blind spots in the deductive analysis of disciplinary perspectives. This analysis implied that we read the full articles when the abstracts did not provide sufficient information on theoretical/disciplinary perspective or methodology.

References

Since abstracts does not allow for the inclusion of references, there is a risk that they will not contain sufficient information on the theoretical and disciplinary perspectives applied in articles. To accommodate this potential bias, we analyzed the references listed in the 204 articles published in *Digital Journalism* from issue 1, 2015 to issue 6, 2018.

This dataset consists of 10,182 references, implying that each article cited on average 50 references. Unfortunately, the references, which we downloaded from Web of Science, were not complete. They included author names, publication year, name of publication, volume (if relevant), page start (if relevant) and DOI handler (if relevant). In addition, author names and publication titles were not spelled in a consistent manner, often also abbreviated differently. For instance, the journal *Journalism Studies* were in some references abbreviated and spelled JOURNALISM STUD, while in others nor abbreviated. Similarly, the same authors appeared with their full name in some references and first names initialized in others. Book titles were also sometimes abbreviated, sometimes not.

Because of these inconsistencies, we had to base the main bulk of the analysis on some kind of unique identifier of sources. The only available identifier was DOI handlers (digital object identifier), which journal articles, proceedings and increasingly digitally published book chapters have. We therefore limited the main part of the analysis to references that contained DOI handlers (41 percent of the references). This means that we had to omit most books, research reports and non-academic sources like newspaper from most of the analysis. However, to secure the validity of this data selection, we did a separate analysis of all publications that were referenced more than 10 times, also including references that did not contain DOI handlers. We manually secured a consistent spelling of these publications.

In addition, we downloaded a database of all scientific journals registered in the Norwegian register for scientific journals, series and publishers.[3] This database contains a categorization of journals in fields and disciplines, which allowed us to determine which fields and disciplines influence digital journalism studies the most.

Findings

We will first present the findings of the analysis of keywords, before we present the abstract analysis and finally the analysis of references. This means that we will not structure the presentation of findings according to the research questions. We will instead use the research questions to structure the Discussion section below.

Keywords and Themes

We were able to identify 11 different thematic clusters from the 1740 keywords (see Table 1). 64 percent of all keywords belong to one of these 11 thematic clusters. 94 percent of all articles have at least one keyword that belong to one thematic cluster. 89 percent of articles have two keywords that belong to a thematic cluster, while 79 percent have three or more keywords that belong to the thematic clusters. The 11 thematic clusters therefore provide an overview of a majority of all articles.

As is visible in Table 1, the most dominant thematic cluster is *Technology*, which was the most dominant thematic cluster in all years, apart from in 2013, when the *Platform* and *Audience* thematic clusters were bigger. The most common clustered

Table 1. Eleven thematic clusters identified through the analysis of keywords in articles published in *Digital Journalism* from issue 1, 2013 to issue 6, 2018.

Thematic cluster	Occurrences in articles in DJ 2013–2018	Share of all keywords	Share of articles with keyword from thematic cluster	Most frequent clustered keywords
Technology	270	16%	48%	digital, data, algorithm, computational, automation
Platform	217	12%	49%	social media, online, mobile, newspapers, multimedia
Audience	180	10%	35%	audience, citizen, participation, public, commenting
Methodology	81	5%	21%	content analysis, survey, comparative, research interview
Theory	75	4%	21%	gatekeeping, agenda, discourse, ANT, field theory
Business	61	4%	15%	business, branding, paywalls, start-ups, management
Region	60	3%	15%	local, global, hyperlocal, Arab spring, United States
Genre	53	3%	15%	long-form journalism, churnalism, narrative, investigative journalism
Philosophy/ epistemology	44	3%	10%	ethics, verification, fake news, epistemology
Visual	36	2%	8%	photography, visual
Professionalism	35	2%	9%	Professionalism, norms, value, role

These 11 thematic clusters account for 64 percent of all 1740 keywords in the 295 articles.

keyword in the technology cluster is, no surprise, "digital", which occurs 55 times. This clustered keyword includes variations like "digital data", "digital technology", "digital journalism", etc. However, "digital" is only the third most common clustered keyword used in *Digital Journalism*. We find the most common clustered keyword within the platform cluster, namely "social media". This clustered keyword (including variations like "Facebook" and "Twitter") occurs 110 times, which is almost twice as many times as the second most popular clustered keyword—"audience"—which occurs 60 times.

Abstracts and Interdisciplinarity

Turning to our analysis of disciplinary perspectives in abstracts (N = 140), we find that they are mostly dominated by sociological perspectives, followed by technological and political science perspectives. These findings are quite similar to the ones reported by Steensen and Ahva (2015) on disciplinary perspectives in *Journalism studies* and *Journalism: Theory, Practice & Criticism*, with two important, but not particularly surprising, differences:

1. A much larger share of the abstracts in *Digital Journalism* is dominated by technological perspectives
2. There is a general tendency that abstracts include a technological perspective in addition to other disciplinary perspectives.

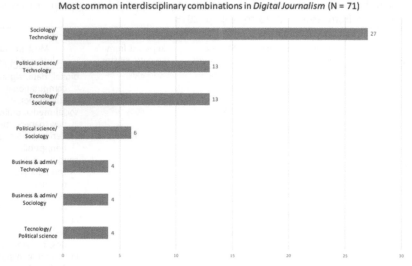

Figure 1. Combinations of disciplinary perspectives in abstracts of articles published in *Digital Journalism* 2013–2018. The figure shows abstracts coded with two almost equally important disciplinary perspectives (71 out 140 abstracts). Numbers must be treated with caution since the N is quite small, and the analysis is quite interpretive, which makes reliability difficult to assess.

This latter point is illustrated in Figure 1, which shows the most common combinations of disciplinary perspectives found in the abstracts. About half of the abstracts analyzed (71) have two almost equally important disciplinary perspectives and most of these combinations were related to sociology and technology.

These sociotechnical abstracts are typically dominated by investigations of the ways in which the digital media environment affects and alters journalistic roles, routines and practices. Examples include Mabweazara (2013), who explores "how the appropriation of the internet and the mobile phone by Zimbabwean print journalists has contributed to a transformation of the profession at a number of levels, including news sourcing routines, and the structuring of the working day"; and Canter (2015), who suggests that "types of Twitter use are diverse but routine practices are forming in the areas of newsgathering and live reporting, causing a shift in traditional gatekeeping and verification conventions".

Political science is the third most common disciplinary perspective in the abstracts analyzed. These articles typically emphasize the political role of news and journalism, foregrounding concepts such as democracy, publics and citizens. Articles within the fourth most common disciplinary perspective, Business and administration, typically focus on business models in the digital age and ways in which the digital media environment poses opportunities and challenges for news media as businesses.

The remaining disciplinary perspectives proposed by Zelizer (2004), including philosophy, culture, history, language, and law, are seldom present in the abstracts. It is for example interesting to note that there are relatively few articles primarily concerned with language. Few studies analyze news content to explore how journalism deals with and reports specific topics—or how news genres evolve or change in the digital media environment. When researchers who publish their work in *Digital*

Journalism analyze text, they tend to do so to find indications of enactments of for instance journalistic roles. We rarely found articles with a primary aim of analyzing textual features of digitally produced news or how the news media deal with specific topics or political debates.

Attitudes Towards Theory

The majority of abstracts do not explicitly mention a specific theory or theoretical framework. These studies seem to build theoretical knowledge based on the sampling of both original and previously published empirical knowledge. This approach resembles a grounded theory approach, which—even though grounded theory is not explicitly mentioned in abstracts—is the dominant approach in more than half of the analyzed abstracts, as was also the case in Steensen and Ahva's (2015) previous analysis. It should be pointed out that the relative lack of theoretical explitness in abstracts does not necessarily indicate that that works published in *Digital Journalism* are theoretically underdeveloped. This lack should arguably rather be seen as an indication of an empirical orientation and theory building in digital journalism studies, taking empirical investigations, rather than theoretical propositions, as its starting point, thus reflecting journalism studies as "a field dominated by a pragmatist-participatory attitude towards theory" (Ahva and Steensen 2019, 78).

However, quite a few articles are conceptual works that introduce new theoretical or methodological propositions for the study of digital journalism. In a closer analysis of the 95 abstracts (and partly also articles) found in issues 1 and 3 of all the volumes of *Digital Journalism*, we found that a relatively large amount of these contributions, almost 40 percent, were either predominantly theoretical contributions, attempts at conceptualization, literature reviews or discussions about research methodology. Some of the most influential articles published in the journal (in terms of citation metrics) are among the ones introducing new conceptual or theoretical frameworks, like Lewis and Westlund (2015) who "argue for developing a sociotechnical emphasis for the study of institutional news production".

The emphasis on conceptual and methodological developments can be interpreted as a sign of a (sub)field in search of its identity. We found a similar sign in the bulk of abstracts that explicitly mention a specific theory or theoretical framework. We identified 59 different theories in the 140 abstracts, which, again, mirrors the theoretical richness found in Steensen and Ahva's (2015) analysis of *Journalism Studies* and *Journalism: Theory, Practice & Criticism*. Sociological theories dominate, with an emphasis on concepts such as institutions, structuration, fields and capital—and more broadly—on perspectives highlighting journalism as an institution and profession, and various forces shaping journalism (i.e., journalistic routines, practices, relations to audiences). This latter includes theories highlighting the relation between humans and technology, such as ANT. Theories from political science are also quite frequent and include theories of citizenship, privacy and surveillance, political economy, and agenda setting.

Apart from ANT and similar sociotechnical theories from STS, there is a lack of theories coming from technology-oriented fields and disciplines like computer science, informatics and information science. This is a bit surprising, given the dominance of technology both as a thematic cluster of keywords and as a perspective in abstracts.

Attitudes Towards Methodology

In our inductive analysis of the 95 abstracts of articles from issues 1 and 3 in all volumes, we also examined the research methods applied. Of those 68 articles that contained some kind of empirical data, we identified 52 that described methods that we classified as social scientific—more than three in four. We included both quantitative and qualitative approaches, from surveys via quantitative and qualitative interviews to observation and field studies.

Methods normally associated with the humanities, such as different kinds of quantitative and qualitative text analysis (image analysis included) were found in 26 abstracts—a little less than four in ten. In other words, there were twice as many articles applying social scientific as humanistic methods. However, only 13 of the articles applied qualitative, humanistic methods. We also found that those articles that claimed to apply methods like qualitative text analysis, discourse analysis, etc., often seemed to do so without applying the research tools commonly associated with humanistic text analysis.

Sources of Influence

The findings so far have revealed that digital journalism studies, as portrayed in *Digital Journalism*, seems quite similar to journalism studies in terms of disciplinary perspectives, theoretical frameworks and methodological approaches, apart from the unsurprising fact that technology has a more prominent place. However, the degrees of interdisciplinarity found so far do not indicate that the orientation towards technology has resulted in disciplinary crossovers between journalism studies and fields and disciplines like computer science, informatics and information science. The final dataset we have analyzed—references in articles published in *Digital Journalism* (from issue 1, 2015 to issue 6, 2018)—may shed some more light on the possible existence of such disciplinary crossovers.

No doubt, articles published in *Digital Journalism* have a variety of sources of influence. Each article cites on average 50 references (listed in the references section). The references with DOI handlers (41 percent) point to 672 different publications, out of which 87 percent are scientific journals, 7 percent are books and book chapter and 7 percent are proceedings. Figure 2 displays the 20 most frequent publications to refer to. These publications account for 63 percent of all references with DOI handlers.

References to articles published in the major journalism journals are most common. The four journalism journals on top account for 36 percent of all references with DOI handlers. It is perhaps no surprise that references to articles published in *Digital Journalism* are most common. Authors need to make sure that their article fits well with the journal's aim and scope and one way of securing this is to build further on research already published in the same journal. However, since *Digital Journalism* is

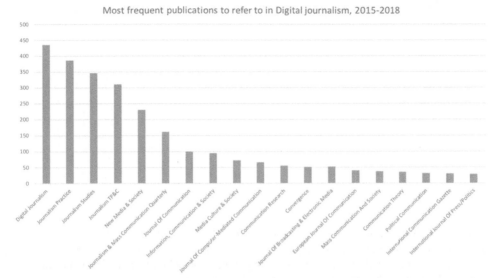

Figure 2. The most frequent journals referenced in all articles published in *Digital Journalism* from 2015 to issue 6, 2018. Based on references with DOI handler only (N = 4125), which account for 41 percent of all references. The top 20 publications account for 63 percent of all references with DOI handlers.

such a young journal, one could have expected that authors would reference other journals with a longer life span to a greater extent.

If we look at the disciplines and fields the publications referenced in *Digital Journalism* belong to, we find that 69 percent of all references with DOI handlers point to publications within the discipline of communication (or "media and communication" as the category is labeled by the Norwegian register for scientific journals, series and publishers).

The remaining 31 percent of references point to publications registered with 47 different fields and disciplines. The Norwegian Register for Scientific Journals categorizes the vast majority (67 percent) of these fields and disciplines as belonging to the social sciences, while 14 percent belong to the category "medicine and health sciences", 12 percent to "natural sciences and technology", and 7 percent to the humanities.

Figure 3 displays the 21 fields and disciplines (apart from media and communications) with 10 or more references in all articles published in *Digital Journalism* from 2005 to 2018 (issue 6).

Publications belonging to library and Information science are the most common source of influence apart from media and communication journals. This discipline account for 9.3 percent of all references with DOI handlers. The most referenced journals within this discipline are *Information, Communication & Society* (95 references) and *Journal of Computer-Mediated Communication* (66 references). The second most influential discipline is psychology, with 3.2 percent of all references with DOI handlers. The most common journals here are *American Behavioral Scientist* (22 references) and *Computers in Human Behavior*.

Because of inconsistencies with the data, the analysis of references presented above only accounts for references with DOI handlers. To check if this limitation obscures the

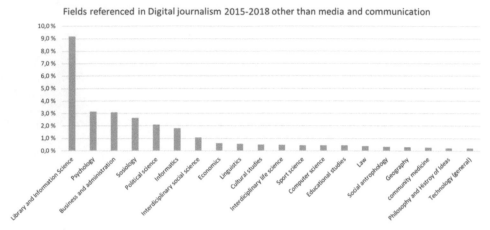

Figure 3. References to publications belonging to other fields and disciplines than media and communication in articles published in *Digital Journalism* from issue 1, 2015 to issue 6, 2018. Only references with DOI handlers are included. Categorization of publications in fields and disciplines follow The Norwegian Register for Scientific Journals. N = 1316.

validity of the analysis, we performed an additional analysis of all publications (journals, books, reports, etc.) that were cited 10 times or more (104 publications), regardless of whether the reference contained a DOI handler or not. Since the spelling of publication names was inconsistent in the data, we manually corrected the spelling of all these 104 publications throughout the dataset. However, for 4 of these 104 publications it was impossible to decide which publications they actually referred to, because the abbreviations could potentially indicate several different publications. We were therefore left with 100 publications that were referenced 10 times or more in *Digital Journalism* from issue 1 2015 to issue 6, 2018. 62 of these publications were academic journals. These journals reflect the analysis of references with DOI handlers above, both in terms of which are the most frequently cited and which disciplines they belong to.

27 of the 100 publications cited 10 times or more were books (without DOI handlers). Since these books potentially offer a different perspective on what influence articles published in *Digital Journalism*, we list them in Table 2.

We can make several interesting observations about the books in Table 2. First, only three of the 27 most cited books were published before 2000. Two of these three books are classical news production studies (Gans 1979; Tuchman 1978), while one is a classical journalism textbook (Meyer 1973). Ten of the books are recent publications (published 2010 or later), thus suggesting a contemporary bias. We find the same bias when we look at the publication year of all references, as 85 percent of them are published post-2000 and more than half (54 percent) are published post-2010. Only seven percent of all references (both with and without DOI handlers) are published before 1990 (N = 10135).

Table 2 also reveals that books discussing aspects related to what we above identified as the audience thematic cluster are quite dominant, as six of the books belong to this theme (Jane B. Singer et al. 2011; Gillmor 2004; Papacharissi 2009; Allen 2013; Napoli 2011; Andén-Papadopoulos and Pantti 2011). Similarly, books that explicitly

Table 2. All books cited 10 times or more in articles published in *Digital Journalism*, issue 1, 2015 to issue 6, 2018. These books account for 10 percent of all publications cited 10 times or more (100 publications).

Book	Times cited
Jane B. Singer et al (2011) *Participatory Journalism*	40
Kari Andén-Papadopoulos and Mervi Pantti (2012) *Amateur Images and Global News*	25
Matt Carlson and Seth C. Lewis (eds, 2015) *Boundaries of Journalism*	22
Herbert J. Gans (1979) *Deciding What's News*	22
Karin Wahl Jørgensen and Thomas Hanitzsch (eds, 2009) *The Handbook of Journalism Studies*	18
Tarleton Gillespie et al (eds, 2014) *Media Technologies*	18
Pablo Boczkowski (2004) *Digitizing the News*	17
Chris Peters and Marcel Broersma (eds, 2013) *Rethinking Journalism*	17
Daniel C. Hallin and Paolo Mancini (2004) *Comparing Media Systems*	16
Henry Jenkins (2006) *Convergence Culture*	15
Chris Paterson and David Domingo (eds, 2008) *Making Online News*	15
Philip M. Napoli (2011) *Audience Evolution*	14
Axel Bruns (2005) *Gatewatching*	14
Gaye Tuchman (1978) *Making News*	14
Rodney Benson and Erik Neveu (eds, 2005) *Bourdieu and the Journalistic Field*	13
Bill Kovach and Tom Rosenstiel (2001) *The Elements of Journalism**	13
Mark Deuze (2007) *Media Work*	13
Pablo Boczkowski and Eugenia Mitchelstein (2013) *The News Gap*	12
Dan Gillmor (2004) *We the Media*	12
Stuart Allen (2013) *Citizen Witnessing*	11
Philip Meyer (1973) *Precision Journalism**	11
Klaus Krippendorff (2004) *Content Analysis**	10
Lawrie Zion and David Craig (eds, 2014) *Ethics for Digital Journalists*	10
Pamela J. Shoemaker and Timothy Vos (2009) *Gatekeeping Theory*	10
Zizi Papacharissi (ed, 2009) *Journalism and Citizenship*	10
Pablo Boczkowski (2010) *News at Work*	10
Bruno Latour (2005) *Reassembling the Social*	10

*The citations of these books refer to several editions of the same books.

deal with the relationship between technology and media/journalism within a socio-technical framework are quite common (Boczkowski 2004, 2010; Boczkowski and Mitchelstein 2013; Carlson and Lewis 2015; Gillespie, Boczkowski, and Foot 2014). Only four of the books can be said to deal with something other than journalism (Latour 2005; Jenkins 2006; Gillespie, Boczkowski, and Foot 2014; Krippendorff 2004), thus strengthening our finding that digital journalism studies, as it is portrayed in *Digital Journalism*, is very enmeshed with journalism studies.

Discussion

The findings presented above reveal that digital journalism studies, as portrayed in the journal *Digital Journalism*, is marked by

- a thematic orientation towards technology, platforms and audiences
- an emphasis on conceptual and methodological discussions
- a participatory-pragmatist attitude towards theory
- a dominance of perspectives and methodological approaches from the social sciences, especially sociology and political science
- understandings and investigations of technology and "the digital" mostly based on sociological frameworks and/or sociotechnical frameworks from the interdisciplinary field of STS

- influences from predominantly journalism studies and the broader discipline of communication, but to some extent also from information science and psychology
- a variety of theoretical perspectives
- a contemporary bias, implying that findings, discussions and conclusions from recent publications (post-2010) might overshadow previously accumulated knowledge

These findings provide answers to the three research questions that guided the analysis of empirical data. Regarding *RQ1: What are the dominant themes and disciplinary perspectives in the journal Digital Journalism?* the answer is to be found in (1) the 11 thematic clusters identified based on keywords, out of which technology, platforms and audiences are the most important and (2) in the analysis of disciplinary perspectives in abstracts, which revealed that sociology and technology are the most common disciplinary perspectives. Moreover, a recurring theme of discussing new conceptual and methodological approaches within digital journalism studies has emerged in the findings. This is no surprise, given the fact that digital journalism studies is a young (sub)field, which—like any other new field or discipline—is likely to search for its identity through theoretical and methodological discussions and, possibly, innovations. However, this is not a finding that makes digital journalism studies any different from journalism studies, as the latter also has been "obsessed with the very definition of its core concept—what journalism is" (Reese 2016, 3).

Diversity Within the Familiar

The second research question—*To what extent and in what ways are articles in Digital Journalism cross- and interdisciplinary?*—has a more complicated answer. Our analysis has searched for thematic, disciplinary, theoretical and methodological diversity. In some respects, digital journalism studies, as it is presented in *Digital Journalism*, comes across as quite diverse. The number of theories identified in abstracts no doubt represents a high degree of diversity, as do the thematic clusters, which range from philosophy to genre studies and technology, thus reflecting disciplinary diversity across the social sciences, humanities and natural sciences.

Yet, the research published in *Digital Journalism* is heavily anchored in journalism studies, as the analysis of both abstracts and references revealed. The diversity of the (sub)field therefore mirrors that of journalism studies, as previously analyzed by Steensen and Ahva (2015). Moreover, even though there is much emphasis on developing new methodological approaches in digital journalism studies, our analysis reveals that the methods actually applied by researchers who publish their empirical work in *Digital Journalism* are not that diverse. (Semi-)quantitative methods from the social sciences dominate.

Diversity in terms of interdisciplinarity seems, at least on the surface, quite high. A variety of fields and disciplines influence the research published in *Digital Journalism*, including most of the familiar ones identified by Zelizer (2004)—sociology, political science, cultural studies, language, history, economy, philosophy, technology and law—but also quite some substantial influences from the disciplines of psychology and library and information science. However, we find it a bit surprising that technological fields and disciplines like computer science and informatics are not more influential. Furthermore, digital journalism studies seems less diverse than journalism studies when it comes to influences from the humanities, as perspectives and (qualitative) methodological approaches from for instance language studies, history and philosophy are almost absent.

We therefore conclude that digital journalism studies, as it appears in *Digital Journalism,* is indeed marked by diversity, but not a kind of diversity that sets it aside of journalism studies. It is diversity within the familiar.

Biases and Blind Spots

Our third and last research question—*What, if any, are the empirical and theoretical biases and blind spots of research published in the journal Digital Journalism?*—provides us with some interesting findings and possible directions for future research. First, digital journalism studies, as it is presented in *Digital Journalism*, has a social science bias, both methodologically and theoretically, which leads to several blinds spots especially related to journalism as a producer of meaning and knowledge in the digital age. Second, digital journalism studies has a contemporary bias, thus neglecting to some extent the legacy of journalism studies. Third, and echoing Boczkowski and Mitchelstein's (2017) argument, digital journalism studies has a blind spot in that it does not include theoretical insights from fields and disciplines like computer science and informatics.

Regarding the social science bias: there are many reasons why journalism scholars should view digital journalism, and other forms of journalism for that matter, predominantly as a social phenomenon. A dominance of social science perspectives and approaches is therefore not in itself a problem. One might even argue that without such a dominance, digital journalism studies would neglect the social, political and to a certain extent cultural ramifications of the digital on journalism. However, approaches from the humanities are also capable of analyzing journalism as a social (and cultural) phenomenon. When perspectives from the humanities are marginalized as they seem to have been with the ways in which digital journalism studies has developed in *Digital Journalism*, and when social science approaches are reduced to (semi-)quantitative methods, crucial elements of digital journalism might be overlooked. The future reader who consults *Digital Journalism* to find out how ideas and discourses were constructed in journalistic texts in the 2010s, how journalism created meaning of and for the societies and cultures it served, how journalism functioned as a system of knowledge creation, and how such questions were connected to historic developments, is likely to be disappointed. To provide answers to such questions, digital journalism studies should to a greater extent embrace the disciplinary perspectives and qualitative methodologies of the humanities.

Regarding the second blind spot, the neglect of historic perspectives, we conclude that digital journalism studies should have a stronger connection with the past in order to better understand the present and predict the future. No doubt, an emphasis on the present is understandable, perhaps even logical, in a (sub)field like digital journalism studies, which to a certain degree is determined to investigate the current changes to its object of study due to recent technological developments. However, this does not mean that such inquiries should only emphasize what is changing, and only look at such changes from the perspectives of recent theories and research. Peters and Carlson (2018, 3) argue that an emphasis on recent changes might "prevent us from questions of material and social power".

Regarding the third blind spot related to the lack of interdisciplinary connections with fields and disciplines of technology, it seems obvious that digital journalism studies should move beyond a topical interest in technology and methods involving skills in computation and the analysis of big data. Digital journalism studies should in addition connect with fields and disciplines like computer science and informatics on a more theoretical level. For instance, the field of theoretical computer science "provides concepts and languages to capture the essence, in algorithmic and descriptive terms, of any system from specification to efficient implementation" (Leeuwen 1990, A: Preface). As digital journalism becomes increasingly dependent on algorithmic processing, acquiring such concepts and languages seems crucial for digital journalism scholarship. Similarly, theoretical understandings of information transformation across natural and engineered systems, which is the essence of informatics as an academic field, seem important for digital journalism scholarship. Practices of digital journalism, especially those related to investigative journalism, are increasingly preoccupied with the analysis of massive amounts of unstructured data, which requires both methodological and theoretical knowledge in order to make sense. Here, digital journalism scholarship needs not only the same kind of knowledge to assess critically such practices of journalism, but also the knowledge to experiment with how digital journalism can make sense of such information transformations. Some examples of the latter already exist, either from within informatics itself, like Wiedemann et al.'s (2018) experimental research on developing tools for the analysis of massive amounts of documents like the Panama Papers or similar big leaks—or from interdisciplinary cooperation like Maiden et al.'s (2018), Nyre's (2015) and Backholm et al.'s (2018) experimentations with new journalistic applications.

Defining Digital Journalism

The empirical articles we have analyzed have one thing in common, in addition to being published in the same journal: They relate to the same object of study, namely digital journalism. If we were to deduce an understanding of this object of study solely based on the empirical research presented in *Digital Journalism*, what would it look like? First, it would not look very different from a definition of traditional journalism, given the similarities between journalism studies and digital journalism studies we have found. Second, it would need to emphasize that digital journalism is predominantly a *social practice* and *institution*, given the dominance of sociological perspectives in the articles published in *Digital Journalism*. Third, a definition of digital journalism based on these articles would have to emphasize the *changing* nature of this social practice and its institutions, changes mostly related to *technology*, *platforms* and conceptions of *audiences*.

Consequently, it is possible to deduce the following definition of digital journalism based on the research published in *Digital Journalism:* Digital journalism is the transforming social practice of selecting, interpreting, editing and distributing factual information of perceived public interest to various kinds of audiences in specific, but changing genres and formats. As such, digital journalism both shapes and is shaped by new technologies and platforms, and it is marked by an increasingly symbiotic relationship with the audiences. The actors engaged in this social practice are bound by the structures of social institutions publicly recognized as journalistic institutions.

This definition relates to digital journalism only as practice and product and does not encompass the types of knowledge digital journalism creates and how this practice and its products functions as a meaning-making system. Nor does the definition give any clues on how digital journalism relates to other social institutions, its cultural implications and questions of power. It is therefore not a definition that grasps everything about digital journalism. It is a definition marked by the biases and blind spots of the research published in *Digital Journalism.*

Limitations

This study is not free from weaknesses and limitations. The most obvious weakness is that we have only analyzed articles published in the journal *Digital Journalism.* Digital journalism scholarship finds it home in many other journals, not to speak of all the books, conference proceedings and reports published each year with relevance to digital journalism research. It is quite likely that we identified the biases and blind spots discussed above because research addressing those biases and blind spots is published elsewhere. However, the journal *Digital Journalism* aims at covering all aspects of digital journalism from a variety of perspectives and methodological approaches, and does not make explicit anything in its self-presentation that would explain the biases and blind spots identified. Also, given the fact that the journal has gained so much impact in so few years, it seems evident that it is a main driver in how the (sub)field of digital journalism studies develops. We therefore feel quite confident that our findings, and our critique, are representative as an analysis of not only the journal, but also of the (sub)field of digital journalism studies.

Our choice of analyzing predominantly metadata and not the actual articles themselves represents a second limitation. We therefore come close to throwing stones while living in a glass house when we critique digital journalism studies for marginalizing perspectives and qualitative approaches from the humanities. We have tried to overcome this limitation to some extent by analyzing abstracts both deductively and inductively and by consulting full articles when we were in doubt. However, future investigations of the metadiscourse on digital journalism studies could benefit from analyzing full articles to a much greater extent. Finally, our content analysis of especially abstracts have some limitations related to its high degree of interpretation and thereby subjective evaluation. We will try to compensate this weakness by making our data publicly available, so that others might do their own analysis—and critique ours.

A third limitation is related to what our metadata included. The data we have analyzed did not include author information like gender, geographic location, age and ethnicity. Future research should look into those other characteristics in search of for instance demographic biases and blind spots and gender issues in digital journalism studies.

Conclusion: The Janus Face of Digital Journalism Studies

We started this article with the observation that digital journalism studies is about to outgrow the field it was established as subordinate to, namely journalism studies. Throughout this article we have consequently labeled digital journalism studies ambiguously as a "(sub)field", thereby not taking a stance on whether digital journalism studies is a field of its own or not. It therefore seems appropriate that we now unmask this ambiguity. Is digital journalism studies a field of its own?

The most logical answer, based on our analysis, is no, digital journalism studies is not a field of its own, understood as having clear boundaries towards other fields. To put it simply; digital journalism studies is journalism studies—with a little twist. Our analysis clearly demonstrates that digital journalism studies, as it is presented in the journal *Digital Journalism,* is well situated in the midst of journalism studies. It is marked by the same kind of diversity and interdisciplinarity as journalism studies and the same attitude towards theory. The largest difference is that digital journalism studies is more preoccupied with technology, the present, and perhaps audiences.

Some of the findings we have presented in this article might seem contradictory, for instance, that research published in *Digital Journalism* is marked by a grounded theory inspired empiricism (label the pragmatist-participatory approach by Ahva and Steensen, 2019) while it at the same time has a strong emphasis on conceptual and methodological discussions. We believe this contradiction constitutes a defining Janus face of digital journalism studies, and we will therefore end this article with some reflections on the possible pitfalls of this two-faced state of the digital journalism research mind.

The Janus-faced state of digital journalism studies is constituted by the following paradox: The research published in *Digital Journalism* is marked by a magnitude of attempts at critiquing old understandings and concepts and developing new. Yet, it seems as if these conceptual discussions have only limited influence on the ways in which researchers analyze their empirical work. Maybe there are too many conceptual discussions going on at the same time, leading to a lack of agreement on which theoretical paths to follow. Since the emphasis of much of the empirical research published in *Digital Journalism* is dominated by things that change and things that are new (like new platforms, technologies, business models and practices), there is a risk that theoretical explanations are rendered unnecessary, perhaps even unwanted. Authors might view theoretical explanations as something that could obscure the possibility to show off whatever new thing the empirical investigation has uncovered. Furthermore, what seems to be new and popular ways of theorizing digital journalism, like for instance ANT, might be, as Benson (2017) argues, just tools to justify that descriptions of empirical findings are more than enough. This, combined with a fascination for quantitative, computational methodology, which in themselves have an anti-theoretical bias and therefore might lead to what Anderson (2008) has called "the end of theory", could lead digital journalism studies on a path to a place where theory has no relevance.

We believe this would be a dangerous path for digital journalism studies to follow, because it would inevitably lead the (sub)field to a place where it loses impact beyond its own boundaries. Fortunately, the conceptual discussions that do go on in *Digital Journalism* (like the ones in this special issue) point to different paths. The challenge is to make empirical investigations follow at least some of the same paths, while also not forgetting the paths that are about to become forgotten and overgrown, namely the ones found within the humanities, and the ones that are more difficult to see, namely those found within theoretical computer science and informatics.

Notes

1. See https://scholar.google.com/citations?view_op=top_venues&hl=en&vq=hum_communication (accessed 13. October 2018).
2. Zotero is an independent open source, free to use reference manager software developed as project of the Corporation for Digital Scholarship and the Roy Rosenzweig Center for History and New Media. It is available at https://www.zotero.org/.
3. The Norwegian Register for Scientific Journals, Series and Publishers is operated jointly between The National Board of Scholarly Publishing (NPU) and The Norwegian Centre for Research Data (NSD) on behalf of the Norwegian Ministry of Education and Research. Located at https://dbh.nsd.uib.no/publiseringskanaler/Forside.action?request_locale=en.

Disclosure statement

No potential conflict of interest was reported by the authors.

References

Ahva, Laura, and Steen Steensen. 2017. "Deconstructing Digital Journalism Studies." In *The Routledge Companion to Digital Journalism Studies*, edited by Bob Franklin and Scott Eldridge II, Chapter 2. London: Routledge.

Ahva, Laura, and Steen Steensen. 2019. "Theory in Journalism Studies." In *The Handbook of Journalism Studies*. 2nd ed., edited by Karin Wahl-Jørgensen and Thomas Hanitzsch. 71–103. London: Routledge.

Allen, Stuart. 2013. *Citizen Witnessing*. Cambridge: Polity Press.

Andén-Papadopoulos, Kari, and Mervi Pantti. 2011. *Amateur Images and Global News*. Bristol: Intellect Books.

Anderson, Chris. 2008. "The End of Theory: The Data Deluge Makes the Scientific Method Obsolete | WIRED." *Wired*. https://www.wired.com/2008/06/pb-theory/.

Backholm, Klas, Joachim Högväg, Jørn Knutsen, Jenny Lindholm, and Even Westvang. 2018. "Tailoring Tools to the Rescue: Lessons Learned from Developing a Social Media Information Gathering Tool." In *Social Media Use in Crisis and Risk Communication*, edited by Harald Hornmoen and Klas Backholm, 185–203. Bingley, UK: Emerald. https://doi.org/10.1108/978-1-78756-269-120181013

Benson, Rodney. 2017. "From Heterogeneity to Differentiation: Searching for a Good Explanation in a New Descriptive Era." In *Remaking the News. Essays on the Future of Journalism Scholarship in a Digital Age*, edited by Pablo J. Boczkowski and Chris W. Anderson, 27–45. Cambridge, MA and London: The MIT Press.

Bijker, Wiebe E. 2009. "Social Construction of Technology." In *A Companion to the Philosophy of Technology*, chap. 15, edited by Jan Kyrre Berg Olsen, Stig Andur Pedersen, and Vincent F. Hendricks, 88–94. West Sussex, UK: Wiley-Blackwell.

Bijker, Wiebe E., Thomas Parke Hughes, and Trevor J. Pinch, eds. 1987. *The Social Construction of Technological Systems: New Directions in the Sociology and History of Technology*. Cambridge, MA: MIT press.

Boczkowski, Pablo J. 2004. *Digitizing the News: Innovation in Online Newspapers*. Cambridge, MA: MIT Press.

Boczkowski, Pablo J. 2010. *News at Work: Imitation in an Age of Information Abundance*. Chicago, IL: University of Chicago Press.

Boczkowski, Pablo J., and Eugenia Mitchelstein. 2013. *The News Gap: When the Information Preferences of the Media and the Public Diverge*. Cambridge, MA: MIT Press.

Boczkowski, Pablo J., and Eugenia Mitchelstein. 2017. "Scholarship on Online Journalism: Roads Traveled and Pathways Ahead." In *Remaking the News: Essays on the Future of Journalism Scholarship in the Digital Age*, edited by Pablo J. Boczkowski and C. W. Anderson, 15–26. Cambridge, MA and London: MIT Press.

Canter, Lily. 2015. "Personalised Tweeting." *Digital Journalism* 3 (6): 888–907.

Carlson, Matt, and Seth C. Lewis, eds. 2015. *Boundaries of Journalism: Professionalism, Practices and Participation*. London and New York: Routledge.

Domingo, David, and Chris Paterson, eds. 2011. *Making Online News: Newsroom Ethnographies in the Second Decade of Internet Journalism*. Vol. 2. New York: Peter Lang.

Eldridge II, Scott A., and Bob Franklin. 2017. "Introduction. Defining Digital Journalism Studies." In *The Routledge Companion to Digital Journalism Studies*, edited by Bob Franklin and Scott A. Eldridge II, 1–12. London: Routledge.

Franklin, Bob. 2013. "Editorial Note." *Journalism Studies* 14 (5): 639–639.

Franklin, Bob, and Scott A. Eldridge II. 2017. *The Routledge Companion to Digital Journalism Studies*. London: Routledge.

Fulton, Katherine, Michael Rogers, and Ellen Schneider. 1994. "What Is Journalism and Who Is a Journalist When Everyone Can Report and Edit News?" *Nieman Reports* 48 (2): 10–13.

Gans, H. J. 1979. *Deciding What's News: A Study of CBS Evening News, NBC Nightly News, Newsweek, and Time*. New York: Pantheon Books.

Gillmor, Dan. 2004. *We the Media: Grassroots Journalism by the People, for the People*. Sebastopol, CA: O'Reilly Media.

Gillespie, Tarlton, Pablo J. Boczkowski, and Kirsten A. Foot. eds. 2014. *Media Technologies: Essays on Communication, Materiality, and Society*. Cambridge, MA: MIT Press.

Harper, Christopher. 1996. "Online Newspapers: Going Somewhere or Going Nowhere?" *Newspaper Research Journal* 17 (3–4): 2–13.

Jenkins, Henry. 2006. *Convergence Culture: Where Old and New Media Collide*. New York: New York University Press.

Krippendorff, Klaus. 2004. *Content Analysis: An Introduction to Its Methodology*. 2nd ed. Thousand Oaks, CA: Sage.

Latour, Bruno. 2005. *Reassembling the Social: An Introduction to Actor-Network-Theory*. Oxford: Oxford University Press.

Leeuwen, Jan. 1990. *Handbook of Theoretical Computer Science*. Edited by Jan van Leeuwen. Vol. A. Amsterdam, The Netherlands: Elsevier.

Lewis, Seth C., and Oscar Westlund. 2015. "Actors, Actants, Audiences, and Activities in Cross-Media News Work: A Matrix and a Research Agenda." *Digital Journalism* 3 (1): 19–37.

Mabweazara, Hayes Mawindi. 2013. "Normative Dilemmas and Issues for Zimbabwean Print Journalism in the 'Information Society' Era." *Digital Journalism* 1 (1): 135–151.

Maiden, Neil, Konstantinos Zachos, Amanda Brown, George Brock, Lars Nyre, Aleksander Nygaard Tonheim, Dimitris Apsotolou, and Jeremy Evans. 2018. "Making the News: Digital Creativity Support for Journalists." In *Proceedings of the 2018 CHI Conference on Human Factors in Computing Systems*, 475: 1–475:11. CHI '18. New York, NY, USA: ACM.

Meyer, Philip. 1973. *Precision Journalism: A Reporter's Introduction to Social Science Methods*. Bloomington: Indiana University Press.

Napoli, Philip M. 2011. *Audience Evolution: New Technologies and the Transformation of Media Audiences*. New York: Columbia University Press.

Nyre, Lars. 2015. "Designing the Amplifon. A Locative Sound Medium to Supplement DAB Radio." *The Journal of Media Innovations* 2 (2): 58–73.

Papacharissi, Zizi, ed. 2009. *Journalism and Citizenship: New Agendas in Communication*. New York and London: Routledge.

Paterson, Chris, and David Domingo, eds. 2008. *Making Online News. The Ethnography of New Media Production*. New York: Peter Lang.

Peters, Chris, and Matt Carlson. 2018. "Conceptualizing Change in Journalism Studies: Why Change at All?" *Journalism*, published online before print 14. May. [CrossRef

Primo, Alex, and Gabriela Zago. 2015. "Who And What Do Journalism?" *Digital Journalism* 3 (1): 38–52.

Reese, Stephen D. 2016. "The New Geography of Journalism Research." *Digital Journalism* 4 (7): 816–826.

Singer, Jane B., Alfred Hermida, David Domingo, Ari Heinonen, Steve Paulussen, Thorsten Quandt, Zvi Reich, and Marina Vujnovic. 2011. *Participatory Journalism. Guarding Open Gates at Online Newspapers*. Oxford: Wiley-Blackwell.

Steensen, Steen, and Laura Ahva. 2015. "Theories of Journalism in a Digital Age." *Digital Journalism* 3 (1): 1–18.

Taylor & Francis. 2015. "Making Your Article (and You) More Discoverable." *Author Services*. http://authorservices.taylorandfrancis.com/making-your-article-and-you-more-discoverable/.

Tuchman, Gaye. 1978. *Making News. A Study in the Construction of Reality*. New York: Free Press.

Turner, Fred. 2005. "Actor-Networking the News." *Social Epistemology* 19 (4): 321–324.

Wahl-Jørgensen, Karin, and Thomas Hanitzsch. 2009. "Introduction: On Why and How We Should Do Journalism Studies." In *The Handbook of Journalism Studies*, edited by Karin Wahl-Jørgensen and Thomas Hanitzsch, 3–16. New York and London: Routledge.

Wiedemann, Gregor, Seid Muhie Yimam, and Chris Biemann. 2018. "New/s/Leak 2.0—Multilingual Information Extraction and Visualization for Investigative Journalism." In *Social Informatics*, edited by Steffen Staab, Olessia Koltsova, and Dmitry I. Ignatov, 313–322. Lecture Notes in Computer Science. Cham, Switzerland: Springer International Publishing.

Witschge, Tamara, C. W. Anderson, David Domingo, and Alfred Hermida. 2016a. "Introduction." In *The SAGE Handbook of Digital Journalism*, edited by Tamara Witschge, C. W. Anderson, David Domingo, and Alfred Hermida, 1–4. London: Sage.

Witschge, Tamara, C. W. Anderson, David Domingo, and Alfred Hermida, eds. 2016b. *The SAGE Handbook of Digital Journalism*. London: Sage.

Zelizer, Barbie. 2004. *Taking Journalism Seriously: News and the Academy*. Thousand Oaks, CA: Sage.

Why Journalism Is About More Than Digital Technology

Barbie Zelizer

ABSTRACT

This article addresses the relationship between digital technology and journalism, arguing that defining journalism in conjunction with its technology short-circuits a comprehensive picture of journalism. Not only does it obscure the incremental nature and detrimental effects of change in journalism, but it sidelines the recognition of what stays stable in journalism across technological change. Tracing the advantages and shortcomings of expectations that digital journalism is more democratic, transparent, novel and participatory, the article argues that it is journalism that gives technology purpose, shape, perspective, meaning and significance, not the other way around.

CONCEPT DEFINITION: Digital Journalism

Defining an entity like "journalism" when it is appended to a qualifier like "digital" necessitates a nod to technology. But how much of a nod is necessary, and what is gained and lost in the exercise?

In this article, I argue that thinking about journalism through its digital apparatus is much like erecting a building while focusing primarily on its exterior. For a structure to function productively as an integral part of the built environment, it needs to partly embrace the architectural mindset of the moment. While computer software designs buildings today in ways not possible in earlier times—with tantalizing suggestions of hypnotic bridges, green power plants and rotating towers—even architecture, often called a science of the future, begins its design with old and proven staples: plumbing, lighting, roofing, support beams. To construct a structure without them ensures its short-lived nature. So too, I argue, does thinking about journalism only through its most recent technological advances.

On Technology's Relevance to Journalism

Separating journalism from its technologies is difficult, because journalism by definition relies on technology of some sort to craft its messages and share them with the public: From bullhorns and alphabets to notepads and cameras, journalists have always used tools to stretch and expand their capacity to collect, document, present and spread information. Journalism's technologies are expansive, resembling an ever-intensifying matrix of new and refashioned capabilities, and they morph assertively, building in both direct and indirect ways on technologies of yore.

Digital technology is no exception. By tweaking and enhancing the qualities of earlier technological environments, the digital magnifies the reach of journalistic practices and output. It hones journalism's focus on acts of compression and extraction, giving new dimensions to what is meant by size, brevity, searchability and retrievability. It amplifies journalism's orientation to speed, and the acceleration, instantaneity and simultaneity that go with it. And it promises increasingly interactive experiences of engagement and in many cases new degrees of affordability.

To be sure, the structural environment surrounding journalism—inhabited by new tech companies, an institutional culture with pervasive power dynamics and patterned structural adjustments to evolving technological parameters—adds to these attributes in directly impacting what digital journalism looks like. Digital technology has introduced marked differences in journalistic style, information-gathering, sourcing, analysis, distribution and financing that have led in turn to new presentational formats: hooks, listicles, gifs, podcasts, virtual and augmented reality, conversational interfaces, data visualization, full immersion experiences, among others. These new formalistic features—enhanced by robust capabilities of storage, retrieval and remediation—make today's news feel more proximate and personalized, usable and interactive than ever before.

Where Technology Falls Short

But the fish story is not the fish, as Carey (1992, 96) famously reminded us. Technology does not become, replace or stand for journalism. Defining journalism in conjunction with its technology often ends up confusing stage with reality, foreground with background, modality with environment. This is problematic for three reasons: it obscures the fact that technology is always incrementally changing journalism; it blinds us to the detrimental effects of technological change; and it fosters forgetting of what stays stable in journalism across changing technological modalities. Ironically, then, despite widespread expectations that technology heightens the human capacity to inform, it does so in ways that eclipse the information relevant to technology's accommodation.

Consider each problem in turn. The focus on what are often called technological revolutions—high points of technological change—facilitates pinpointing, ranking and ordering, comparing and inventorying an enterprise's unique and adaptive technological traits. But it can also foster a facile understanding of how change alters what used to be. Though the idea of fast change is compelling, most enduring change unfolds in bits and pieces, with no technology ever staying the same for long. Recognizing change, however, tends to herald discrete high moments after multiple small changes have already occurred, making its identification—and celebration—into a post-hoc and somewhat arbitrary marker of what happens gradually.

This makes it easy to sidestep the long and continuous nature of innovation and the recognition that all technologies build in some way on those that came before. How much attention in journalism is typically given to the arrival of paper, maps, batteries, fax machines, telephones, tape recorders, ballpoint pens, transistors or GPS?

Each has changed journalism in fundamental ways. Because journalism's past is focused instead on the discussion of large technological inventions—the telegraph, camera, radio, TV, cable, laptop, wireless—that sought to overhaul the journalistic enterprise and promised different expectations of how news would be made and consumed, the story of journalism and technology has generally been told as a skip across grand technological moments, the most recent of which is digital in nature. It is no surprise, then, that digital technology is widely hailed as changing the fundamental contours of journalism and its relationship with the public. Each new large technological advancement in journalism has been received as a matter of course as if civilization were about to begin from anew, even as it wipes away the ongoing and incremental nature of technological change.

Secondly, applauding journalism's technological dimensions can distract attention from existing deficits. They are worth repeating, if only for the simple reason that not recognizing them simplifies one's grasp of technology and magnifies its celebration in unjustified ways. Journalism's accommodation to technology has long constituted its largely unremarked backdrop, where dividing journalism by its technological attributes has been one way of addressing the intricacies of technological change. Those teaching journalism skills readily demarcate the enterprise by technological tools, separating broadcast from print or photography from radio, and that pedagogical stance by and large persists even as the current embrace of multi-tasking forces more technological blending than in the past.

The entrenchment of technological divides plays into technology's celebration as advancing the broader journalistic enterprise, pivoting toward a continued separation of digital journalism from its neighbors. It also fosters a preference for practitioners who are technologically agile in each silo. Digital journalists are expected to have some appreciation for multiple outcomes of technology that have not been a traditional part of a journalist's tool box: social networks, multi-media, big data, mobility, analytics, metrics, to name a few. But what gets less discussed is what is not necessarily digital journalism's forte, as Shafer (2016) sagely observed: important experiences relevant to the meaning-making that accompanies what he called journalism's "reading real estate," including hesitation, focus, a sense of completeness, surprise, chance, deeper comprehension, fidelity and contemplation. Experientially, we are left with the more limited kind of engagement that Shafer likened to driving toward a destination rather than walking there. One gets us where we want to go faster, but we lose much information, context and sensory experience along the way. In his words, "news is best sipped like whiskey, not chugged like beer."

Finally, much about journalism remains stable across adaptive technologies. But the attention given stability fades when primary investments continue to focus on the latest technological revolution. News relay that is faster, sleeker, more captivating, interactive, immediate and personalized might conjure up various forms of involvement, distraction or entertainment but it still needs to be recognized as news at day's end. Its collection through many but not all of the same impulses that have driven journalism from its inception—curiosity, independence, a sense of adventure and enterprise, serendipity, exploration, creativity, resourcefulness, a flair for writing—tend not to be centrally mentioned as part of what makes a good digital journalist. And indeed, their under-emphasis in digital journalism leaves unclear how journalistic craft will continue to fare as time moves on. Too often digital enterprises act as if being digital and online constitutes the full spectrum of relevant journalistic skills. That elision may help explain why so much of current news falls short in covering the multiple political, economic and social ills that plague today's increasingly dark times.

The stability of journalism's core—the idea that individuals associated with certain recognized and reliable enterprises are entrusted with collecting and disseminating information for the public good—matters. Its present disregard makes journalists into unwilling and uneven contestants in the race for attention and ends up supporting those who contend that all journalism is up for grabs. It is often said that journalists are resistant to change, but perhaps what they resist more is the diminution of their craft that often comes with it.

Defining Digital Journalism

So how do we define digital journalism? Most nods to the "digital" involve some combination of four interconnected expectations, interpretive impulses that assume that digital journalism is more democratic, transparent, novel and participatory than earlier technologies in the news. Any definition should begin with these expectations, but it needs to do so by complicating the largely celebratory rhetoric surrounding them with a somewhat more somber review of their limitations.

Expecting digital journalism to somehow democratize the publics that it serves draws from broad expectations surrounding journalism itself, heralding journalism's oft-cited relevance to democratic life. Across time, the story of journalism's technologies has largely been told as one that is progressively instrumental to democracy, making information available to growing numbers of people from increasingly different walks of life and geographic regions. In digital journalism, notions of the network society, its flattened hierarchies and openness, its orientation toward deinstitutionalization and deprofessionalization, and its increased participation and personal agency are widely thought to enhance the democratic function, giving more voice to people who formerly had little or none.

But expectations of democratic access and sharing for all have been unevenly realized in digital technology (Hindman 2008). The still persistent digital divide, thin discussion of structural inequities, disinterest in participation among digital users coupled with a cacophonous struggle for attention, siloed algorithms and, most importantly, for-profit nature and advertising's dominance of digital content all complicate the democratic aspirations related to digital journalism (Peters and Witschge 2015). Moreover, the digital's celebrated flattening of authority obscures both the nature of authority in pre-digital and non-digital modalities and the possibility that some structure—hierarchical, institutional or professional—might be a good thing. As Shafer (2016) noted, journalism's design hierarchy is an intricate responsive display to evolving patterns of production and consumption over time.

Transparency in digital journalism is widely seen as a way to ensure the trust, credibility and legitimacy associated with the news. By disclosing journalism's intricate

workings, impulses of transparency help link digital practitioners to the most fundamental notions of journalists as honest brokers of truth (Deuze 2005). Because journalists' use of digital technologies is seen as a way for them to be upfront about their
practices, transparency helps mitigate the discomfort accompanying technology's role
as a substitute for human action. But despite the fact that calls for transparency have
been widely connected with the promise of digital technology, that promise has not
borne out evenly (Diakopoulos and Kolista 2017). As anonymity plays a growing role
in digital content, for instance, digital innovations are increasingly blurring the line
between fantasy and reality, making it hard to discern transparency both initially and,
due to the impermanence of digital content, over time.

Though transparency was associated with the earliest moves toward the digital,
digital journalism has now become the unhappy home to a whole set of practices in
which the staged and inauthentic look deceptively real, as the monikers of fake news,
post-truth and alternative facts suggest. Moreover, assuming a linkage between digital
technology and transparency erroneously suggests that there is no transparency in
pre-digital and non-digital journalistic settings.

Impulses associated with novelty come with the territory of any enterprise needing
to keep pace with the changing parameters of external forces. Though novelty and
innovation are not restricted to technology (Steensen 2011), journalism has always
been at least partly oriented to technological innovation, and the digital is no exception (Boczkowski 2005). But an emphasis on the new makes it easy to forget or under-
state similarities between many of the newer outlets on journalism's horizon and
those in journalism's past. Parallels are being struck repeatedly across digital and pre-
digital technologies: podcasts and radio, Buzzfeed and the newswires, infographics
and bar charts, Snapchat's Discover feature and old media news feeds. Though recent
advances in journalism's core practice—investigative reporting—led to the publication
of both the Panama and Paradise Papers because hundreds of journalists worldwide
collaborated on the digital analysis of leaked documents, such collaboration goes on
all the time in newsmaking, even if on a different scale and scope.

Moreover, much about journalism's orientation to the present and future tends to
sidestep its ongoing nod to the past, an ahistoric bias that has long characterized
journalistic engagement. Not recognizing that novelty needs the familiar and already-
tried to contextualize what novelty means has created a fixation on the new that
undermines the understanding of current events (Zelizer 2016). How much of today's
news about authoritarianism, populism and immigration, for instance, could be more
productively understood via a fuller nod to history? And yet the woefully thin presence of the past in current news weakens or even prevents the development of such
comprehension.

Expecting digital journalism to enhance user participation is built into journalism's
broader role in fostering the public good. Assumptions that an engaged or participatory news user is a responsible citizen help position digital participation as journalism's
latest manifestation of its service to the public (Lewis 2012). But celebrating a participatory set of users does not necessarily take into account what kind of engagement
ensues (Singer et al. 2011). Nor does it address the full range of experiences associated
with participation: digital cues that promote offline behavior, ongoing digital feedback,

participation in particular conversations, all online interactions, to name a few. The different social structural positions of individuals and groups and their consequent varying degrees of access are also left largely unexplored.

Furthermore, the widespread reliance in digital journalism on a certain kind of audience metrics—exemplified by clicks, pageviews, likes, shares, retweets and followers—leaves unclear how to discern or measure participation. As its invocation in digital journalism ranges across sheer digital activity, time spent on particular sites, comprehension, learning and social mobilization, it is clear, as Poindexter (2012) pointed out in her study of millennial news users, that engagement without a connection to broader values often leads to disengagement and disinterest. Additionally, participation's celebration in digital spheres makes it seem erroneously as if pre-digital and non-digital participation is an anomaly.

What each of these impulses suggests is that the celebration of the "digital" in digital journalism offers much of value. But it also unnecessarily creates binaries where they need not be, binaries that appear to position democracy, transparency, novelty and participation on one side of a technological spectrum that aligns with digital technology. The positioning of these binaries is important to consider because the affirmative response to each binary pair adheres to and bolsters the efforts by which journalism strives to position and sustain itself as an enterprise worth preserving. Which kind of journalism, including digital, would want to dissociate itself from embracing the democratic, transparent, novel and participant dimensions of collective life? Setting the digital aside, however, many of the impulses currently driving its celebration have long been at the forefront of journalism's sense of self, regardless of technology.

Thinking about the digital, then, is as much about what we think we want from journalism as it is about offering nuanced definitions of what the digital is. Aspirations that journalism can continue to be more democratic, transparent, novel and participatory, despite the instability of increasingly dark conditions for journalism's operation, provide a ray of hope in an otherwise gloomy projection of times ahead.

With expectations of a better life pivoting in large part on technology, journalism's digital mode is the most recent but not the only conduit for imagining an optimum link between the news and the broader collectivity. Following a long line of technological modalities that have offered journalism the chance to address its continued viability, the "digital" in digital journalism is a modality not an environment, a foreground not a background, a stage not reality. It is on these terms that the "digital" provides journalism with the opportunity to play out its ongoing existential and definitional struggles.

How Can Journalism and Technology Connect More Fruitfully?

All of this suggests that thinking about journalism primarily through technology risks separating our understanding of the news from its broader historical legacy, geographic variations, and social, cultural, economic and political contingencies. Admittedly, this article regards journalism more through the lens of its occupational practices and output than the structural and other institutional entities that impact its shaping. But without correcting the disjunctions that ensue when occupation meets technology, we risk obscuring what should remain journalism's raison d'etre: the ability to independently cull and develop new and original information. How much repurposing of old information—so called "evergreen content"—occurs alongside fresh coverage, not only at Business Insider and Vox but also at FiveThirtyEight and The Awl? How much does original and independent news-gathering drive or even figure into current evaluations of digital journalism?

At a point in time when journalists face threats and intimidation across the globe, original and independent news-gathering should be our most prominent cue for reminding us what any kind of journalism, including digital, needs to be about. For though it constitutes only one dimension of journalistic practice, it acts as a litmus test for thinking about journalism more broadly.

Importantly, original and independent newsgathering occurs in types of journalism that bear little similarity to the impulses most actively driving discussions of digital journalism. The creative and autonomous collection of news unfolds with varying impact in journalism that is more and less democratic. We see it in journalism whose content displays varying degrees of transparency and opaqueness. We find it in journalism that regularly mixes new and old technologies in attempts to ensure a message's delivery and comprehension. And it surfaces in journalism that dictates, moralizes, preaches and teaches even as it engages more active participation.

What does this suggest about the relationship between "digital" and "journalism"? Despite repeated claims that the digital will save journalism from extinction, the opposite may be true. Returning to the architectural metaphor with which this article began, the digital remains the exterior of the journalistic enterprise, and regarding it as journalism's savior is much like saying that a structure's exterior surface will ensure the building's success, plumbing and lighting be damned. Like other enterprises that have been transformed by digital technology, such as education, the market, law and politics, it is the enterprise—journalism—that gives technology purpose, shape, perspective, meaning and significance. Digital technology is not immune to this view, regardless of how compelling it might be. Ultimately, I define digital journalism in the following way:

> Digital journalism takes its meaning from both practice and rhetoric. Its practice as newsmaking embodies a set of expectations, practices, capabilities and limitations relative to those associated with pre-digital and non-digital forms, reflecting a difference of degree rather than kind. Its rhetoric heralds the hopes and anxieties associated with sustaining the journalistic enterprise as worthwhile. With the digital comprising the figure to journalism's ground, digital journalism constitutes the most recent of many conduits over time that have allowed us to imagine optimum links between journalism and its publics.

Those who are concerned about the shape of journalism's future need to be more thoughtful about what place we give technology in thinking about the news. If journalism is to thrive productively past this technological revolution and into the next, we need to do better in sustaining a fuller understanding of what journalism is, regardless of its technological bent, and why it matters. For that revolution, like the many before it, will surely come.

Disclosure statement

No potential conflict of interest was reported by the author.

References

Boczkowski, Pablo. 2005. *Digitizing the News*. Cambridge, MA: MIT Press.

Carey, James W. 1992. *Communication as Culture*. London, UK: Routledge.

Deuze, Mark. 2005. "What Is Journalism? Professional Identity and Ideology of Journalists Reconsidered," *Journalism* 6 (4), 422–464.

Diakopoulos, Nicholas and Michael Kolista. 2017. "Algorithmic Transparency in the News Media," *Digital Journalism* 5 (7), 809–828.

Hindman, Matthew. 2008. *The Myth of Digital Democracy*. Princeton, NJ: Princeton University Press.

Lewis, Seth. 2012. "The Tension between Professional Control and Open Participation," *Information, Communication & Society* 15 (6), 836–866.

Peters, Chris, and Tamara Witschge. 2015. "From Grand Narratives of Democracy to Small Expectations of Participation," *Journalism Practice* 9 (1), 19–34.

Poindexter, Paula. 2012. *Milennials, News and Social Media: Is Social Engagement a Thing of the Past?* New York, NY: Peter Lang.

Shafer, Jack. 2016, 10 September. "Why Print News Still Rules," *Politico*. https://www.politico.com/magazine/story/2016/09/newspapers-print-news-online-journalism-214238

Singer, Jane B., Hermida, Alfred, Domingo, David, Heinonen, Ari, Paulussen, Steve, Quandt, Thorsten, Reich, Zvi, and Vujnovic, Marina (2011). *Participatory Journalism*. New York, NY: Wiley-Blackwell.

Steensen, Steen. 2011. "Online Journalism and the Promises of New Technology," *Journalism Studies* 12 (3), 311–327.

Zelizer, Barbie. 2016. *What Journalism Could Be*. Cambridge, UK: Polity Press.

The 5Ws and 1H of Digital Journalism

Silvio Waisbord

ABSTRACT

Digital journalism is the networked production, distribution, and consumption of news and information. It is characterized by networked settings and practices that expand the opportunities and spaces for news. Digital journalism is the outgrowth of new ecological conditions for the circulation of news content in contemporary society and the crumbling of the pyramidal model of news that prevailed since the beginnings of industrial journalism. These unprecedented developments have broadened the essential elements of journalism—the who, what, where, when, why, and how news are reported.

CONCEPT DEFINITION: Digital Journalism

Digital journalism (DJ) has become a multipurpose keyword in journalism studies. A rich trove of journals, books, and reports attests to the enormous difficulties of producing a synthetic, integral definition of DJ (Witschge et al. 2016). It is a protean concept. It is the name of a line of research and practice articulated around developments driven primarily by technological changes (Franklin and Eldridge 2017; Karlsson and Sjøvaag 2018). It denotes a radically new phase in the history of journalism primarily brought about by the digital revolution. It has become an expedient shorthand to refer to a distinctive set of questions and trends at the intersection of technology and journalistic practice. It is associated with innovative forms of producing and distributing news as well as news engagement and participation: blogging, data, and computational journalism, social media news, algorithm, hyperlocal, and mobile news. So much is folded under "digital journalism" that no succinct definition could do justice to a diversity of theories, concepts, and attributes.

What is digital journalism then? Does it refer to all forms of journalism in "the digital society"? Is all contemporary journalism "digital journalism"? What is journalism? What is the "digital society" anyway? Any effort to define DJ quickly bumps into unresolved semantic disputes over the meaning of "journalism" and "digital."

We are past the time when "digital" was primarily identified with specific formats, platforms, or the coding and storing of information (Grueskin, Seave, and Graves 2011). In the past two decades, unending controversies over the defining aspects of "the digital" in contemporary societies have added additional several layers of meaning (Lupton 2014). As either adjective or noun, the meaning of "digital" goes beyond a matter of information coding into 0s and 1s, or particular software and hardware. It is neither just about the specific properties of data nor the attributes of information technology. Instead, "the digital" represents the rise and the consolidation of networked forms of social action facilitated by technological innovations. Understood as networked social action, "digital" foregrounds institutional and structural transformations in journalism and news. It is about revolutionary changes in social and public life articulated through the Internet rather than about specific attributes of information and technologies.

Likewise, "journalism" remains the subject of long-standing definitional battles among journalists, academics, observers, and policy-makers (Vos 2018). Some believe it a distinct occupation focused on reporting and commentary about current events performed by salaried workers ("journalists") who typically toil for corporations ("news/journalistic organizations"). Others believe journalism is a particular set of occupational practices that follow certain *public ethics* in the production of news and information that makes *meaningful* contributions to public life, society and/or democracy. Finally, others espouse the notion that any act of producing news about current events is journalism.

Where does this leave us to define digital journalism? My option is to marry preferred meanings of each concept – digital as networked social action, and journalism as the reportage of news and information. *Digital journalism is the networked production, distribution, and consumption of news and information about public affairs.* What is distinctive about DJ are networked settings and practices (Domingo and Wiard 2016; Russell 2011; Ryfe 2016) that expand opportunities and spaces for reporting news. DJ broadens conventional understandings of journalism and news - who produces daily information for large-scale consumption as well as what is socially considered and used as news. DJ is the outgrowth of new ecological conditions for the circulation of news content in contemporary society that resulted from the crumbling of the unidirectional, pyramidal model of industrial journalism and the consolidation of more flattened conditions for public expression. Journalism was primarily organized around the production of news by newsrooms and news companies that relegated citizens to minor roles. This model has not completely collapsed; it remains viable, active and influential notably in legacy news organizations. Yet it currently exists in a completely different environment of networked actors, information abundance and chaos, and multidirectional communication flows.

The 5Ws and 1H of digital journalism

To discuss the specificities of DJ, I repurpose the classic 5Ws and 1H questions of journalism as an analytical device.

Who: Virtually anyone with access to the Internet can take part in digital journalism. No longer are journalists and newsrooms the only suppliers of news, information, and commentary. A vast array of actors contributes massive amounts of news content (Lewis and Westlund 2015). News is not only what "journalists" decide. Ordinary citizens, once thought simply as "passive audiences," are busier than ever. They produce, share, snack, click, scan, modify, and comment on news for public consumption. Fact-checking companies work with social media and news organizations. Public relations and marketing firms have perfected the science of news virality and native advertising. Government agencies flood the Internet with content that resembles traditional news. Activists' groups and non-government organizations constantly churn out information for public consumption. Crowd-produced news are ubiquitous in websites and social media. Global networks of journalists and citizens collaborate in investigate stories. Social media algorithms shape news offerings and display. In summary, although not everyone fits conventional definitions of "journalist," anyone can potential play one on the Internet.

The explosion of journalistic fare produced by multiple actors has upended the traditional division of labor between news producers and users – journalists and the rest of society. This disruption of news roles has unsettled the modernist notion of news authorship grounded in firm and stable relationships between production and output. Certainly, non-journalistic actors were never passive actors, quietly expecting newsrooms to decide the news and uncritically digesting reams of news. Yet news conditions have profoundly shaken up the "who" of news. Authorship is not only embedded in networks of countless *produsers* who compete for space and attention with journalists and newsrooms. News authorship is also more complicated as networks of authors permanently produce layers of content by adding, discussing, excising, deleting, and reframing content. The authenticity of news is thrown into question when many authors produce digital news feeds.

Purists reasonably doubt that anyone who reports and comments news on the Internet is truly a journalist. They continue to uphold the idea that journalists are those who report news following standard professional principles and get compensated for performing a regular job (Carlson and Lewis 2015; Coddington 2014). One may not think that news and commentary produced by non-journalistic actors are journalism *strict sensu*, or believe that conventional journalistic organizations are on equal social standing and influence with armies of news *produsers*. Yet news content produced by various sources is socially used as news, without concern or care about origin and legitimacy. Multiple authors contribute content to platforms that function as news sources, such as social media feeds, streams of commentary appended to news articles, and scattered satirical news. Who is a digital journalist is under dispute (Ferrucci and Vos 2016) as digital journalism makes everyone a potential source of news.

Another important issue that not all *produsers* have similar power. Notably, legacy news brands, digital giants, major news-makers and well-resourced corporations have a dominant presence in terms of recognition, capacity to produce news, and reach. These are hugely important differences considering the constant fight for public atten-tion. The fact that digital journalism features new actors who had a marginal presence in the past does not mean that it has ushered in horizontal, egalitarian conditions. Huge disparities persist based on long-standing inequalities in market access, political influence, and economic muscle of individual and collective actors.

What: The content of digital journalism can be anything. Stock-in-trade products of industrial journalism included news, commentary, opinion, headlines, letters to the editor, arts reviews, obituaries, and interviews. To this content, digital journalism has added a plethora of content: social media postings, memes, readers' comments and reviews, blogs, podcasts, satire, hoaxes, rumors, and fake news. As a consequence of the proliferation of content, news and information goes beyond traditional journalistic criteria. DJ is not particularly tied to any strict epistemology or conventional news routines and norms to decide what makes news. Certainly, one could reasonably argue that industrial journalism has also featured diverse offerings – highbrow and tabloid content, in-depth investigations on important matters and trivial happenings, quality reporting and puff pieces. Despite the consolidation of professional ideals, it was never unified by a single logic, a set of criteria to establish news content. Yet DJ offers an even wider range of content that blends personal and institutional information, private and public issues, fact and fiction.

Where: DJ happens in a variety of platforms that are not limited by geography, language and other barriers that historically circumscribed journalism's place and reach. Whereas journalistic content was delivered through channels/media such as newspapers and broadcast news, DJ takes place anywhere on the Internet. Content is published and accessed in different formats and platforms. Websites, search engines, and social media applications as well as personal computers and mobile platforms are the gateways to DJ. Partnerships between legacy news organizations and Facebook, content specifically targeted to certain national and global audiences, and editions in multiple languages, are just some examples that reflect changing practices in terms of where news are accessed. Despite the reluctance of social media companies to be considered information providers, they do act as journalistic organizations: they have become main platforms for regular access to news and information and regulate flows of content according to corporate objectives.

When: DJ has blown up modern notions of time in news production and consumption. Industrial journalism built regimented and distinct notions of time both in the definition of news (When did something newsworthy happen?) and the consumption of news (When were newspaper and broadcast editions made public?). These understandings shaped journalistic notions about "news cycle" and "deadlines" as well as the manufacturing of "news audiences" in specific time slots (Bødker 2017). Old time-bound conventions of news production and delivery persist in industrial journalism, but time works differently in DJ. DJ is characterized by the constant circulation of news. Content is changed and complemented by revisions and updates in traditional news platforms. News feeds are regularly updated. 24-7 information replaces a regimented series of time-bounded production (deadlines) and consumption (editions). News are on anytime.

Why: The purpose of DJ ("why make news") is much broader than in modern journalism. Journalism featured news and other content for many reasons: to create audiences for advertisers, to make money, to scrutinize and to support power, to champion partisan causes, to educate and influence the public, to create visibility for influential newsmakers. In contrast, DJ represents many more purposes. Multiple actors have many motivations to participate in news-making. Individuals are driven by information, self-presentation, and social connection and support. Companies pursue corporate branding and reputation fixing. Social media corporations set to make money and drive up profits. Social activists want to make demands and change policies and public opinion. Political propagandists spread news to deceive voters. Legislation mandates government agencies to disseminate news and information.

How: How news are reported also sets DJ apart from journalism. Journalism traditionally had a more defined set of procedures and norms to produce content. Typically, reporters follow news routines, values, and sources to find stories and had to meet organizational expectations crystallized in codes of ethics and informal rules. Journalists learned these competencies in schools and on the job. News organizations streamlined occupational behaviors through stylebooks, training, and feedback. As an occupation with professional ambitions (Waisbord 2013), industrial journalism tried to maintain jurisdictional control over the provision of news and daily information through formal and informal work regulations. Certainly, traditional journalistic organizations have not given up of such goals, as they continue to observe occupational norms as well as their content on social media and readers' comments.

In contrast, DJ lacks similarly well-defined and agreed-upon principles. It can be described as a Far West of news rules and a Babel of news-making discourses. It is a free-for-all environment without clear, shared rules about "how" content should be produced and distributed. It is antithetical to strict regulations and formalized procedures. There are not streamlined guidelines or enforced principles about how information should be reporters in the wild world of digital journalism.

Digital journalism is networked journalism

What explains the characteristics of digital journalism and its differences with industrial journalism? The consolidation of new institutional conditions - sprawling technology-enabled networks, that connect news-making actors. Certainly, networks and connectivity are not new to journalism. Industrial journalism had been immersed in multi-levelled networks, too. It never existed alone, perfectly suspended in air, unbounded by any social force, free to do as it wished. Quite the opposite. Journalism has historically been embedded in webs of informational, economic, political, and cultural forces and maintained relations with myriad actors: governments, corporations, advertising and public relations firms, industrial and editorial interests, socio-cultural trends, audience preferences. These interests shaped journalism as a whole as well as specific news organizations – the nodes of networks that influenced the features of newsrooms: content, funding, style, format, editorial positions.

The networks of DJ, however, are far more complex, open, noisy, and unruly. They include overlapping and multiple interests that coalesce around many forms of reporting – professional and citizen, industrial and post-industrial, evenhanded and partisan, paid and free, fact and factless, hyperlocal and global, commercial and non-commercial. It features "news active" citizens and organized groups. "Participation in news" (Peters and Witschge 2015) may not necessarily have virtuous democratic consequences, as some predicted in the earlier days of the Internet, but it adds more news *producers*. It also brings to the fore the growing power of platforms, notably Facebook and Google, for news access, production, and dissemination.

Given superposed, shapeshifting networks of *producers*, content, and platforms, blurred boundaries are intrinsic to DJ. In the old days of the mass media, journalism attempted to demarcate boundaries vis-à-vis many social interests, at least during its shining moments when it pursuit public interests. It tried to separate the wheat of news from the chaff of information, gossip, rumors, propaganda, and commercial persuasion. No doubt, it frequently failed to do so as it passed lies, unverified information, spin and pap for news. But the professional ideal of journalism was filled with democratic promise and principles that called for sustaining boundaries vis-à-vis virtually anyone – governments, corporations, publics, advertisers, sources, bean counters. Press laws glorified independence. Professional canons prized distance. Journalistic ethics praised autonomy. Accolades rewarded distance from power in order to hold the powerful accountable.

Industrial journalism has drawn from professional ideals to reinforce boundaries as digital journalism constantly ignores and blurs lines. Journalism has reacted with a mix of distrust and caution to armies of parvenus that produce news and that serve as news sources such as citizen journalists and social media corporations. It carefully opened the door to new forms of news and commentary – from citizen journalism to readers' input out of fear of damaging professional reputations and corporate brands. Newsrooms insist on affirming the difference between facts and truth, journalistic genres and formats, real and fake news, news and propaganda as a host of impostors and journalistic wanna-bes flood the Internet. Journalists criticize Facebook for blurring lines between news and advertising (Moses 2018). Even journalistic upstarts with a different sensibility for news, such as Buzzfeed, continue to uphold professional ethical principles (Tandoc and Foo 2018).

A steadfast defense of canonical professional ideals is not surprising. Incumbent professions and powerful institutions are not exactly generous towards rowdy developments that unsettle and threaten the existing order. They do not graciously give up or share power. They do not voluntarily open the gates of the Bastille to welcome upstart revolutionaries for a cup of coffee to discuss peaceful coexistence. Professional journalism has been no exception. Just like systems theorists, it fervently believes in functional specialization, differentiation, and re-differentiation. Like Smithian economists, it firmly praises the positive contributions of the division of labor. The reasons are many: from self-serving goals (maintain authority and credibility) to public-oriented motivations (protect news from spurious interests).

Professional journalism sticks to its ideals and practices that emerged at a time when it was the gravitational center of a hierarchical and centralized information architecture. A blend of modernist values (truth, transparency, rationality, facticity, freedom) still anchors the collective imaginary of newsrooms. They provide the ideological standing points from where professional journalism reacts to developments in digital journalism and tries to reposition itself *après la revolution*. It confronts a twofold challenge: the viability of those principles when the institutional architecture that grounded industrial journalism has crumbled, and the compatibility between its core principles and the complex networks at the core of digital journalism driven by multiple motivations.

Journalism's penchant for drawing boundaries uneasily fits the networked nature of DJ, which lacks neat and stable boundaries (Loosen 2015). DJ comprises various types of journalism. Straight reporting and opinion, confirmed facts and invented assertions, half-hearted truth-telling and plain deception, information and persuasion exist side by side. Social media seamlessly blend news with commercial advertising and propaganda. Non-professional news actors ignore journalistic conventions. Readers consume absolute fictions as if they were (f)actual representations of reality, and engage with news without much concern for the identity or the legitimacy of the source. Rogue actors spread false information. All are mixed up in the noisy disorder of news. Unlike journalism loyal to the professional ideal, the many actors of digital journalism are not mindful of boundaries. They do not seem to be extremely worried about drawing boundaries to protect news from external influence or to bolster their *bona fides* as public-minded guardians of daily information.

Multiple forms of news content are infused by different set of concerns, demands and goals. No news *produser* has full control over dispersed webs of news. Interdependence prevails in networked environments. No single logic, principle, or ethics dominates digital journalism. Decentralized and open networks connect scores of actors who hold widely different epistemologies, values, and motivations. These attributes set digital journalism apart from newsroom-based, industrial journalism.

Conclusion

What are the implications of the innovations of DJ for journalism studies?

First, "the digital" should not be narrowly understood in terms of tools and hardware. To state the obvious, the potential and the uses of "digital technologies" is news reporting and dissemination are important. They offer new opportunities to gather and analyze reams of data, to inform comprehensively, to investigate power, to engage with multiple publics, and to tell multi-sided stories. But not every newsroom fully taps into the potential of technological innovations. Digital technologies may not immediately change the ways newsrooms organize and approach news coverage – newsgathering routines, news values, and news sources. Funding, corporate strategies, work organization, and newsroom cultures shape the way technologies are incorporated.

Second, it is important to place the study of professionalism in journalism in shifting network structures and dynamics. Several questions should be considered. How does industrial journalism interact with digital journalism? How does it try to secure its social standing while engaging with the bottomless information churned out by digital journalism? How does it integrate and domesticate the constant flow of news and information? Does digital journalism push changes in the traditional news values and ethical norms of newsrooms?

Finally, organizational studies of journalism need to contend with broader theoretical and empirical questions. Traditionally, this approach was focused on news routines and professional norms that organize newswork internally and connect newsrooms with external actors – governments, public relations firms, advertisers, civic society organizations, social movements, neighborhoods, communities. Today, industrial journalism exists amid a complex web of actors who are not only interested in engaging with newsrooms to make news, but they are also active in news production. Understanding how it navigates a crowded, shifting field of news sources is necessary to analyze inertia and changes in the industrial organization of newswork.

In closing, DJ challenges industrial journalism in many ways. It presents opportunities and threats. Just as it offers possibilities for newsrooms to tap into a wealth of information and to engage with multiple publics, it has also thrown industrial journalism off its dominant position. By doing so, it pushes the latter to reassess its connections to social actors, to adapt to new circumstances, and to revalidate its social standing and power when news are everywhere. Digital journalism also pushes scholarship to open the analytical lens in order to examine a range of networked practices that happen beyond newsroom-centered, industrial production of news.

References

Bødker, Henrik. 2017. "The Time(s) of News Websites." In *The Routledge Companion to Digital Journalism Studies*, edited by B. Franklin and S. A. Eldridge II, 55–63. London, UK: Routledge.

Carlson, Matt, and Seth Lewis (Eds.). 2015. *Boundaries of Journalism: Professionalism, Practices and Participation*. New York, NY: Routledge.

Coddington, Mark. 2014. "Defending Judgment and Context in 'Original Reporting': Journalists' Construction of Newswork in a Networked Age." *Journalism: Theory, Practice & Criticism* 15 (6): 678–695.

Domingo, David F., and Victor Wiard. 2016. "News networks." In *The SAGE Handbook of Digital Journalism*, edited by Tim Witschge, C. W. Anderson, D. Domingo, and A. Hermida, 397–409. Thousand Oaks, CA: SAGE.

Ferrucci, Patrick, and Tim Vos. 2016. "Who's in, Who's out?." *Digital Journalism* 5 (7): 868–883. doi: 10.1080/21670811.2016.1208054.

Franklin, Bob, and Scott A. Eldridge II. Eds. 2017. *The Routledge Companion to Digital Journalism Studies*. London, UK: Routledge.

Grueskin, Bill, Ana Seave, and Lucas Graves. 2011. *The Story so Far: What We Know about the Business of Digital Journalism*. New York, NY: Columbia University Press.

Karlsson, Michael, and Helle Sjøvaag. 2018. *Rethinking Research Methods in an Age of Digital Journalism*. London: Routledge.

Lewis, Seth, C., and Oscar Westlund. 2015. "Actors, Actants, Audiences, and Activities in Cross-Media News Work: A Matrix and a Research Agenda." *Digital Journalism* 3 (1): 19–37.

Loosen, Wiebke. 2015. "The Notion of the "Blurring Boundaries": Journalism as a (de-) Differentiated Phenomenon." *Digital Journalism* 3 (1): 68–84. doi:10.1080/21670811.2014.928000.

Lupton, Deborah. 2014. *Digital Sociology*. London, UK: SAGE.

Moses, Lucia. 2018. (June 11). Seven News Organizations Protest Facebook's Issue Ads Policy. *Digiday*. Retrieved from: https://digiday.com/media/seven-news-organizations-protest-facebooks-issue-ads-policy/.

Peters, Chris, and Tamara Witschge. 2015. "From Grand Narratives of Democracy to Small Expectations of Participation: Audiences, Citizenship, and Interactive Tools in Digital Journalism." *Journalism Practice* 9 (1): 19–34. doi:10.1080/17512786.2014.928455.

Russell, Adrienne. 2011. *Networked: A Contemporary History of News in Transition*. Cambridge: Polity.

Ryfe, David. 2016. News Institutions. In *The SAGE Handbook of Digital Journalism*, edited by T. Witschge, C. W. Anderson, D. Domingo, and A. Hermida, 370–382. Thousand Oaks, CA: SAGE.

Tandoc, Edson, C., and Cassie Yuan Wen Foo. 2018. "Here's What BuzzFeed Journalists Think of Their Journalism." *Digital Journalism* 6 (1): 41. doi:10.1080/21670811.2017.1332956.

Vos, Tim. (Ed.). 2018. *Journalism*. Boston/Berlin: DeGruyter.

Waisbord, Silvio. 2013. *Reinventing Professionalism: Journalism and News in Global Perspective*. Cambridge: Polity.

Witschge, Tamara, C. W. Anderson, David Domingo, and Alfred Hermida (Eds.). 2016. *The SAGE Handbook of Digital Journalism*. Thousand Oaks, CA: SAGE.

Digital Journalism as Symptom, Response, and Agent of Change in the Platformed Media Environment

Jean Burgess ⓘ and Edward Hurcombe ⓘ

ABSTRACT

This article brings together perspectives from digital media studies and journalism scholarship to propose a working definition of digital journalism that can guide scholarship and applied research in this field. We define digital journalism as "those practices of newsgathering, reporting, textual production and ancillary communication that reflect, respond to, and shape the social, cultural and economic logics of the constantly changing digital media environment." We elaborate and illustrate this definition through a discussion of the co-evolving relationship of journalism with the Internet and social media platforms since the 2000s and outline in detail how social news outlets such as *BuzzFeed* are paradigmatic examples of these dynamics and relationships. The article concludes by emphasizing the urgent need for both the study and practice of digital journalism in the public interest, especially in the context of an increasingly platformed and closed media system. We focus particularly on the methodological challenges and threat to public oversight that recent moves to platform enclosure and lockdown represent and provide some suggestions as to how these might be addressed.

CONCEPT DEFINITION: Digital Journalism

Introduction

Digital journalism might have once been a niche topic, but these days, it is everybody's business. The ongoing challenges around news media business models, as well as the role of the Internet in misinformation, algorithmic distribution and organised anti-social disruption in social media platforms are of significance and concern to society as a whole. Consequently, digital journalism is now of interest to a range of social science, humanities and even science and technology disciplines – from political communication through to sociology and digital media and communication; extending to new transdisciplinary formations around data science and machine learning, as we discuss towards the end of the article. But first, we bring together our own disciplinary backgrounds in digital media and journalism studies to offer a perspective on what digital journalism is, why it matters, and how it might be studied.

In offering our own interdisciplinary contribution to the conversation, we first want to emphasise the multi-sided structure of the digital media industries (Wikström 2013), and consequently, the co-evolutionary dynamics of digital transformation. This co-evolutionary approach is especially crucial in any study of the media industries, since media forms, platforms and practices play such an important role in shaping the public understanding and acceptance of technological change. The social shaping of technology (MacKenzie and Wajcman 1999) and mutual shaping of technology (Boczkowski 2004) approaches have come to play an influential role in digital media and Internet studies over the past decade, including through commonly used theoretical formulations such as "social media logics" (van Dijck and Poell 2013), which we draw on here and have used in our (2018) discussion of the new forms and formats of "social news".

Accordingly, we want to highlight how journalism not only symptomatically *reflects*, but also pragmatically *adapts to* and *influences* the changing media environment. Formally, we propose to define digital journalism as

> Those practices of newsgathering, reporting, textual production and ancillary communication that reflect, respond to, and shape the social, cultural and economic logics of the constantly changing digital media environment. To study digital journalism, then, is to study the transformative and isomorphic impacts of digital media technologies and business models on the practices, products, and business of journalism; to interrogate the ways that journalistic discourses, practices and logics in turn shape the cultures and technologies of those digital media platforms through which journalism is practiced and its products are shared and consumed; as well as to identify and amplify the opportunities for new forms and practices of journalism to *intervene* in this increasingly platformed digital media environment.

These dynamics and relationships have become more visible and important alongside the growing significance of the Internet since the 1990s, and with the advent of the platform-dominant social media paradigm since the mid-2000s. The ideologies and politics of journalism in the context of digital media have transformed significantly over this period, with the role and future of digital journalism reaching a point of crisis and urgency in the late 2010s, just as social media platforms have become more powerful and more politicised than ever before.

Early in the development of the web and social media, particularly with the rise of "serious" political and news blogging in the early to mid-2000s, there was much hype about the Internet-led democratisation of journalism. Associated with blogging was an ideology of openness and accessibility that would break down the divisions between – or at least stimulate new relationships among – professional journalists and ordinary citizens. The promised shifts were, implicitly, technologically driven: under the logic of convergence, the affordances of the digital reduced the barriers to news production, reducing the industrial and formal distinctions that had separated journalism from oral and everyday news-sharing practices like conversation, or gossip, or letter-writing. There was much optimism: about the future of journalism as a participatory practice that would not necessarily be bound to the fate of traditional news organisations; and about the potential for diverse forms of niche journalism made viable through the increasingly distributed news consumption environment (Bruns 2008).

Skipping ahead more than a decade, any remaining allure of the Web 2.0 model has been overshadowed by the near-global dominance of a small number of proprietary digital platforms – a situation we have discussed elsewhere as the "platform paradigm" (Burgess 2015). As such platforms have commercially matured and formalised, while the onward *sharing* of content is more than encouraged as part of consumption, there has been a steady reinscription of the separation between content production and consumption roles – through the policing of copyright, for example; and through different structures for participation on the platforms in question. Additionally, in practice, it is evident that the concept of journalism and the figure of the journalist (as opposed to writer, blogger, contributor, or poster) remain deeply entangled with the industrial structures and routines of news and media organisations – whether large or small; long-established or just starting up; and whether commercial, public-service oriented, or community-driven – even when these structures and routines are undergoing digital transformation. Hence, for the remainder of this contribution, we focus primarily on the nexus between journalism understood as a quasi-professional practice conducted in relation to some kind of news media organization, and the changing digital media environment.

Doing journalism, digitally

Digital journalism commonly refers to new genres and modes of journalistic storytelling that exploit the interactive multimedia affordances of digital media technologies and the Internet, the journalistic use of digital and data-driven investigative and reporting methods, or some combination of these. Data-driven digital storytelling techniques were highlighted in an award-winning 2017 story by the Australian Broadcasting Corporation (ABC), the national public service media organisation, which used voting data to create an interactive map of the results of Australia's same-sex marriage postal survey (Liddy, Hoad, and Spraggon 2017). The news story here was visualised on a broad national scale, but also offered opportunities for personalisation – with users able to breakdown the vote by state and electoral division, according to their own interests. Digital video has also emerged as a significant element in new modes of reportage and storytelling, pioneered by outlets like *Vice News*. *Vice* was notable in the early 2010s for gonzo-like videos tackling edgy subjects like illicit drugs, extreme body modifications in Asia, and North Korea, drawing on the amateur aesthetics, intimate relations, and youthful cultures of YouTube to great success (Bødker 2017). These *Vice* videos typically featured young people reporting on their own experiences as they flung themselves into the heart of dangerous situations or exotic locales, and thus they also drew on the ethos of citizen journalism and participatory media, adapting existing news forms to the logics and cultures of emerging social media platforms like YouTube.

Doing journalism digitally can also mean new ways of gathering news within the digital media environment, whether sourcing stories from Twitter using "social listening" methods (hence bringing together Internet research methods with journalistic techniques), or simply by using a range of digital technologies for interviewing, documenting and gathering information. Twitter's inbox feature, for instance, is now frequently used by journalists as a way to gather news tips-offs and to source quotes for stories. Tweets themselves commonly feature in digital news stories, and have come to perform a number of functions. At times their role is in the tradition of television news vox-pops (that is, as a curated representation of public opinion), at others they are used as a way to add colour or humour to a news story, with embedded tweets acting as a kind of "best of Twitter" on the topic or event that is the focus of the story. In the case of public figures, embedded tweets can function as interactive quotes straight from the source, or as the object of news stories themselves. Social media and Internet culture is now itself a regular beat for some journalists, especially in the light of the recent concerns around disinformation, political manipulation and hate speech, and the platform governance challenges around dealing with these issues, on Facebook, Twitter and YouTube (Gillespie 2018). *BuzzFeed* has once again proven to be a pioneer in this field, producing, for instance, important investigative work into the cultures and political manoeuvrings of far-right Facebook groups, and the role of the newsfeed algorithm in intensifying them (Broderick 2017).

Digital journalism is bound up with new ways of distributing news and reaching audiences using the interactive and conversational affordances of social media platforms. Twitter in particular allows journalists to be accessible to their readers – with journalists using the platform to not only promote and share their work, but also to engage other users, be they readers or other journalists, in frequently informal ways. Here, the personalising logics of Twitter and the platform's emphasis on conversation have helped foster sociable and intimate online personae for journalists, as well as providing a space for them to connect to, debate and support each other. At the same time, some news outlets and media companies – especially born-digital outlets like *BuzzFeed* – actually require journalists to have an active and visible Twitter presence, and this imperative to be active on the platform – as part of and in addition to their more traditional news work routines – has raised concerns about the ever-expanding labour demands of the profession. Moreover, as journalistic work grows increasingly insecure, Twitter has become a central part of the entrepreneurial journalist's toolkit: a Twitter profile is crucial in developing and promoting a personal brand, which can be taken from job to job, and in the case of freelance journalists, from story to story. Facebook pages, too, can be spaces for journalists and other writers to share their work and foster discussion and debate – notwithstanding the toxic comment culture of the platform, especially on contentious or polarising political issues.

Finally, the power of platforms in defining the metrics for and algorithmically shaping audience engagement has attracted industry and academic concern. As news outlets and media companies came to rely heavily on individual platforms – especially, in English-speaking and most European contexts, Facebook and Google – such companies have become vast repositories of granular data, allowing them to see the clicks or shares of individual articles or videos in real time, linked to demographic and other personal and relational attributes; with attention shaped in the first place by the often opaque algorithms used to curate and present the content to users (e.g., through the Facebook newsfeed). Packaged metrics based on this data are typically provided to publishers and page owners in graphic or simplified tabular form by the platforms. Publishers, news organisations and journalists may have little sense of why one story gains more attention than another, but their institutional practices, values and priorities may become increasingly responsive to these metrics anyway, hence mirroring the priorities and values of the platforms themselves, in a process of "institutional isomorphism" (Caplan and Boyd 2018).

For instance, in the early-to-mid 2010s, Facebook valued clickthrough rates and likes and shares over engagement time (that is, time spent on a webpage directed away from Facebook). This led to an explosion of "click-bait", characterised by the use of attention-grabbing and sometimes misleading headlines designed to induce users to click through to an article, regardless of whether it held any interest for them once there. In an effort to combat click-bait, Facebook in 2013 and 2014 retuned their newsfeed algorithm to favour what they called "high-quality" content, where quality was defined by whether users continued to engage with the news content continuously after they clicked on it, and also took into account the average time spent on the content away from Facebook; thereby incentivising the publication of "long reads" and rich media content. Concurrently, the desire for more precise metrics, and analytics that help publishers to interpret and use them, have produced a somewhat lucrative market for intermediaries that can provide analytics software and expertise to news outlets (Belair-Gagnon and Holton 2018). While metrics provide a greater understanding of reader tastes and interests, there nonetheless remains a degree of uncertainty within news outlets about what kinds of stories and content will be successful. Iteratively releasing news onto platforms, seeing what "the algorithm" does with it, and reshaping the content accordingly (even in real-time through A/B testing), have become routine practices of digital journalism.

Digital journalism as symptom and response: the case of social news

We now zoom in on the close symbiotic relationship between social media platforms on the one hand, and popular, born-digital styles of journalism, as exemplified by outlets such as *BuzzFeed*, on the other. Social news, we argue, can help scholars better understand contemporary transformations in news and journalistic practice in relation to the logics and cultures of social media platforms.

We have extensively discussed this sub-genre of digital journalism elsewhere under the rubric of 'social news', which we frame as a distinctive genre with shared characteristics, all of which result from this mutually constitutive relationship between new forms of journalism and the logics of social media (Hurcombe, Burgess, and Harrington 2018). Although the term "social news" had appeared earlier in journalism scholarship in reference to news-sharing platforms like (the now defunct) Digg (Wasike 2011), our term specifically refers to the shareable characteristics and explicit "positionality" of an emerging genre of news associated with born-digital outlets like *BuzzFeed* (the most well-known example), the Australian-based *Junkee* and *Pedestrian.tv*, and others. This genre is distinguished by a fluency in the vernacular conventions and pop-culture sensibilities of social media: that is, the acronyms, the memetic imagery, and the affective uses of GIFs (frequently depicting celebrities) common to platform cultures. This fluency in turn helps to boost the shareability of these outlets on platforms whose business models rely on sharing and social connection among users.

The other key feature of social news, positionality, can be understood as emerging out of platform-based social justice politics. By positionality we mean the ways that these outlets transparently position themselves within issues and stories, explicitly demonstrating consistent support of and identification with primarily politically progressive causes, rather than adopting a speaking position at a distance from the action and above the fray – as traditional norms of journalism objectivity dictate. This positionality does not necessarily pose a threat to journalistic integrity. Instead, it can not only help engage certain readers through explicit identification with causes – and thus enhance shareability – but also actually address ongoing issues associated with the normative discourse of journalistic balance (Boykoff and Boykoff 2004), which has increasingly been exploited by far-right groups in order to gain airtime or column space and thus lend legitimacy to their views. In fact, the social news outlets we studied regularly critiqued the dangerous political impacts of major Australian outlets performing this kind of "false balance", and giving airtime to neo-Nazis, for example (Hurcombe, Burgess, and Harrington 2018).

It builds on and directly references Twitter's call-out culture, which refers to the practice of publicly identifying instances of problematic behaviour or language use online. The practice of "calling out" problematic content is important community and platform moderation work that has fallen disproportionately to women of colour, queer people and racial minorities (Nakamura 2015), but that social media-based journalists are also taking up. Positionality can also be understood as a commercial response to the increased economic viability of microtargeting, as Facebook and Twitter allow outlets to promote themselves to highly specific audiences using demographic and post-demographic criteria. Social news, therefore, is a good example of digital journalism as symptom of and response to the logics and cultures of the platformed digital media environment.

Digital journalism as an agent of change

The dynamics of social news we have sketched above show how digital journalism is shaped by the digital media environment. But, to return to the latter part of our initial definition of the concept, social news also shows that journalistic practices, institutions and values have a shaping effect on digital media platform cultures, thereby endowing journalism as a practice and as a field of study with some agency in, and indeed responsibility for, the changing media environment. This influence goes beyond niche publications like *Buzzfeed* and *Junkee*, however. Here we could point to the transformation of Twitter from an interpersonal status update tool to a global newsroom (Burgess 2015); a process of legitimisation largely driven by media coverage and the enthusiastic adoption of the platform by journalists and news organisations. We can point to the various forays by Facebook into editorial intervention and curatorial decision-making, both automated and human-centred. As indicated by the click-bait example above, Facebook has had to adjust its algorithmic infrastructure and explicitly acknowledge its increasingly interventionist editorial role – in deciding what is and is not valuable news content; in signalling contested news, harmful content, and misinformation after news content had become popular on the platform in the early 2010s.

Thus, despite their protestations to the contrary, social media platforms have indisputably crossed the line from being perceived as neutral intermediaries to being media organisations with significant influence over public communication (Napoli and Caplan 2017). With this transition has come public and regulatory pressure for them to take on roles and responsibilities with respect to content curation and moderation – activities they have long undertaken in the interests of retaining users and pacifying advertisers, but which are increasingly expected to take place in the public interest and with public oversight, despite the contested nature of both the public and its interests (Gillespie 2018) – thus bringing them into the sights of journalists. These issues came to a head for Facebook with the widely publicised Cambridge Analytica scandal (in which millions of Facebook users' personal data gathered a deceptive quiz was harvested and used for the purposes of political manipulation), and related incidents of deliberate trolling and interference in political news and campaigning via social media leading up to and following the 2016 US Presidential election – a complex story that was uncovered through the assiduous investigative efforts of digitally literate journalists working in traditional news organisations like *The Guardian*, provoking widespread public and regulatory concern, and prompting Facebook to announce significant changes to their policies and practices with respect to user privacy.

As the cultural, social and economic logics of the digital media environment change, so too will digital journalism; and journalism has a role to play in not only highlighting and questioning, but also shaping, the trajectory of these changes. It is only by attending to the changing technological affordances and business models of digital media platforms that digital journalism can be both studied and practiced in the public interest – that is, for us, in service of an open society, civic values and human rights. Increasingly, this will mean both researchers and journalists having access to the digital traces of how digital media platforms are curating and moderating news content and user interactions around it. Making use of these data requires both journalists and researchers to acquire the tools and capabilities necessary to interrogate these platform practices through a range of digital methods, by which we mean more specifically the appropriation of "the methods of the medium" (Rogers 2013) in order to investigate or critique that medium or platform. Such methods include large-scale analyses of tweets, various kinds of algorithmic audits (Sandvig et al. 2014), and, increasingly, the development of forensic computational techniques necessary to identify and tackle misinformation, from tracking the deliberate spread of rumours to uncovering and reverse engineering video "deep fakes" using generative adversarial networks (Chesney and Citron 2018).

However, the opportunities for concerned social actors to use these kinds of digital methods for the purposes of public oversight of the digital media environment are rapidly diminishing as platforms move to lock down data access. These moves have been happening most visibly since the late 2000s, partly as part of a broader transition away from the Web 2.0 ideology of open innovation, towards increased centralisation and the concentration of media power within a small number of proprietary platforms; and partly as part of the growth of social media data markets (Burgess and Bruns

2015), which produces a disincentive for platforms to provide data access on anything other than a commercial basis.

A series of moves was undertaken by major proprietary platforms including Facebook, Instagram and Twitter in early 2018 to shut down third-party access to data – not only to personal user data, but data on how content is curated, shared and engaged with on their services. While the platforms' public statements suggest that the changes were aimed at improving data security and user privacy (see, for example, Schroepfer [2018]), these developments perversely threaten to have a chilling effect on reporting and research into the very issues of misinformation, filter bubbles, and inappropriate content that are of most public concern with respect to these platforms (for further, detailed discussion of how such lockdowns threaten research and critique, see Bruns et al. 2018). If it is true, as the well-known and frequently lampooned *Washington Post* masthead slogan goes, that "democracy dies in darkness", it is essential that society retains the ability to shine the light on and interrogate the legitimacy and fairness of the operations of these platforms, which after all coordinate and govern so much of our media environment, our everyday communication, and our political processes (Suzor 2018). There has never been a more important moment for investigative, forensic and technologically savvy digital journalism research and practice; it is imperative, therefore, that the international community of scholars, practitioners and activists with an investment in the future and trustworthiness of digital journalism keep up investigative and policy pressure on the interlocking issues of platform governance and transparency. Arguably the most important role for digital journalism, then, is as an agent of change within the constantly changing digital media environment of and to which it is both a symptom a response.

Disclosure statement

No potential conflict of interest was reported by the author(s).

ORCID

Jean Burgess http://orcid.org/0000-0002-4770-1627
Edward Hurcombe http://orcid.org/0000-0002-5838-2019

References

Hurcombe, E., J. Burgess, and S. Harrington. 2018. "What's Newsworthy about 'Social News'?: Characteristics and Potential of an Emerging Genre." *Journalism* (in press).

Burgess, J. 2015a. "From 'Broadcast Yourself' to 'Follow your Interests': Making Over Social Media." *International Journal of Cultural Studies* 18 (3): 281–285.

Burgess, J., and A. Bruns. 2015b. "Easy Data, Hard Data: The Politics and Pragmatics of Twitter Research after the Computational Turn." In *Compromised Data: From Social Media to Big Data*, edited by G. Langlois, J. Redden, and G. Elmer, 93–111. London: Bloomsbury.

Belair-Gagnon, Valerie, and Avery E.Holton. 2018. "Boundary Work, Interloper Media, And Analytics in Newsrooms." *Digital Journalism* 6(4): 492–508.

Bødker, Henrik. 2017. "Vice Media Inc.: Youth, Lifestyle – and News." *Journalism* 18 (1):27–43.

Boykoff, Maxwell T., and Jules M.Boykoff. 2004. "Balance as Bias: Global Warming and the US Prestige Press." *Global Environmental Change* 14 (2):125–136.

Boczkowski, Pablo J. 2004. "The Mutual Shaping of Technology and Society in Videotex Newspapers: Beyond the Diffusion and Social Shaping Perspectives." *The Information Society* 20 (4):255–267.

Broderick, Ryan. 2017. "I Made a Facebook Profile, Starting Liking Right-Wing Pages, and Radicalized My News Feed in Four Days." BuzzFeed News, 8 March. https://www.buzzfeednews. com/article/ryanhatesthis/i-made-a-facebook-profile-started-liking-right-wing-pages-an.

Bruns, Axel. 2008. *Blogs, Wikipedia, Second Life, and Beyond: From Production to Produsage.* New York: Peter Lang.

Bruns, Axel. 2018. "Facebook Shuts the Gate After the Horse Has Bolted, and Hurts Real Research in the Process." Internet Policy Review. https://policyreview.info/articles/news/ facebook-shuts-gate-after-horse-has-bolted-and-hurts-real-research-process/786.

Caplan, Robyn, and Danah Boyd. 2018. "Isomorphism Through Algorithms: Institutional Dependencies in the Case of Facebook." Big Data and Society. http://journals.sagepub.com/ doi/full/10.1177/2053951718757253.

Chesney, Robert, and Danielle KeatsCitron. 2018. "Deep Fakes: A Looming Challenge for Privacy, Democracy, and National Security." 107 California Law Review (2019, Forthcoming); Univ. of Texas Law, Public Law Research Paper No. 692; Univ. of Maryland Legal Studies Research Paper No. 2018–21. doi:10.2139/ssrn.3213954.

Gillespie, Tarleton. 2018. *Custodians of the Internet: Platforms, Content Moderation, and the Hidden Decisions that Shape Social Media.* New Haven: Yale University Press.

Liddy, Matthew, Nathan Hoad, and Ben Spraggon. 2017. "How Australians Think About Same-Sex Marriage, Mapped." ABC News, 13 September. http://www.abc.net.au/news/2017-09-13/ same-sex-marriage-support-map-vote-compass/8788978.

MacKenzie, Donald, and Judy Wajcman, Eds. 1999. *The Social Shaping of Technology. No. 2nd.* Buckingham, UK: Open University Press.

Nakamura, Lisa. 2015. "The Unwanted Labour of Social Media: Women of Colour Call Out Culture as Venture Community Management." *New Formations: A Journal of Culture/Theory/ Politics* 86:106–112.

Rogers, Richard. 2013. *Digital Methods.* Cambridge, MA: MIT Press.

Napoli, Philip, and RobynCaplan. 2017. "Why Media Companies Insist They're Not Media Companies, Why They're Wrong, and Why it Matters." *First Monday* 22 (5): doi:10.5210/fm.v22i5.7051.

Sandvig, Christian, Kevin Hamilton, Karrie Karahalios, and Cedric Langbort. 2014. "Auditing Algorithms: Research Methods for Detecting Discrimination on Internet Platforms." *Paper presented at International Communication Association*, Seattle, May. http://social.cs.uiuc.edu/ papers/pdfs/ICA2014-Sandvig.pdf.

Schroepfer, Mike. 2018. "An Update on Our Plans to Restrict Data Access on Facebook." *Facebook Newsroom*, 4 April. https://newsroom.fb.com/news/2018/04/restricting-data-access/.

Suzor, Nicolas. 2018. "Digital Constitutionalism: Using the Rule of Law to Evaluate the Legitimacy of Governance by Platforms." Social Media + Society. doi:10.1177/2056305118787812

van Dijck, José, and ThomasPoell. 2013. "Understanding Social Media Logic." *Media and Communication* 1 (1):2–14.

Wasike, Ben S. 2011. "Framing Social News Sites: An Analysis of the Top Ranked Stories on Reddit and Digg." *Southwestern Mass Communication Journal* 27 (1):57–68.

Wikström, Patrik. 2013. "The Dynamics of Digital Multisided Media Markets." In *A Companion to New Media Dynamics*, edited by JohnHartley, JeanBurgess and AxelBruns,231–246. London: Wiley Blackwell.

Locating the "Digital" in Digital Journalism Studies: Transformations in Research

Sue Robinson, Seth C. Lewis (iD) and Matt Carlson (iD)

ABSTRACT

This essay applies six commitments for journalism studies to research involving digital technologies, namely: contextual sensitivity, holistic relationality, comparative inclination, normative awareness, embedded communicative power, and methodological pluralism. We argue that the emergent characteristics of digital journalism – as reflected in algorithms, automation, networking tools, and mass posting, sharing, and production with a click of a button – bring on transformations that must be theorized holistically, contextually, and relationally as part of a subfield of journalism studies called "digital journalism studies." Spatial and temporal considerations inform this argument and complicate how the field of journalism studies examines news production and consumption. It is within the studies of "transformation" that we as researchers find an emergent theory that not only reveals the disruption of norms and introduction of new developments, but also exposes enduring power dynamics. By locating the "digital" in digital journalism studies through the lens of these six commitments, scholars can better identify evolving and blurring boundaries of news content and its production, distribution, and consumption processes.

CONCEPT DEFINITION: Digital Journalism

The term "digital" is at once obvious and confusing, as evidenced by ongoing debates over definitions: What exactly is meant by "digital"? Is technology a useful synonym? Isn't all journalism now "digital"? Is the word itself now unnecessary? What happens when the "digital" we know is inevitably replaced by nanotechnology or another "post-digital" technology (Peters 2016)? These questions provide the foundation for this essay, which is meant to provoke the ongoing scholarly conversation about the usefulness of *journalism studies* as a distinct field within the larger communication discipline as well as the particular place of *digital* as a point of concern and orientation. In seeking to organize a formal appreciation of "digital journalism studies" as a subfield of "journalism studies," we build theory around the concept of "transformation."

The starting point is our recent article attempting to draw boundaries around what makes journalism studies distinct (Carlson et al. 2018). In it, we argue that the burgeoning field of journalism studies could be framed according to six commitments: contextual sensitivity, holistic relationality, comparative inclination, normative awareness, embedded communicative power, and methodological pluralism. This essay applies that framework to the notion of *digital* journalism studies. We define "digital" here as the modes of production that transcend the temporal and spatial constraints of analog media, with their particular physical limitations of production and distribution.[1] *Digital* brings entry into a networked communicative world where computer programming allows for what Singer (2018: 216) calls an "immersive, interconnected, individualized, iterative, and instantaneous" experience of news consumption. Appending the word *digital* locates technology as an artifact for research to foster an understanding of its processes and impact through the deep exploration of news production, consumption, content, and distribution, all considered in various ways holistically, contextually, and relationally. Digital journalism studies, then, encompasses how the news media ecology is being reconstituted by mobile technology, social media, and other digital platforms, enabling what scholars have called "ambient" news that is omnipresent in our lives (Hermida 2010) as well as "networked" news wherein a reporter's notebook and other physical-world artifacts of a geographically oriented newsroom can go viral (Steensen and Ahva 2015). This subfield of journalism studies, at least as it has been evolving in relation to new technologies, narrows the scope of scholarship in digital journalism studies to the realm of online news production, distribution, consumption, information networking, manipulating, and sharing.

We use this essay to call for a rethinking of "digital" as representative of "transformation" – that is, a continuous mode of change that must be theorized alongside the acknowledgment that the only certainty is uncertainty and constant metamorphosis, in ways applicable for journalism particularly and for humanity broadly. Such ephemerality includes disruption of existing institutional and organizational norms but also eruption that brings forth something(s) entirely new. It is within the studies of transformation that we see how digital capacities (e.g., interactivity) and immersive attributes (e.g., virtual reality) alter experiences across different platforms. Furthermore, in these emphases on transformation, we can identify structural, social, and other kinds of continuity that persist at varying levels of analysis.

We aggregate these characteristics into a three-part definition of *digital journalism studies*:

- Research that involves newswork employing digital technologies in some manner, such as news websites, social platforms, mobile devices, data analytics, algorithms, etc.;
- Research that acknowledges how digital dynamics of journalism interact with and alter formerly discrete boundaries such as work and play, old and new, and private and public, as well as geographic spatialities, past/present/future temporal realities, producer/distributor/consumer actors, and the authority and forces that go along with these changes and configurations;

- Research that interrogates the resulting practical and cultural transformations occurring around news and other acts of journalism as they relate to broader issues such as the maintenance of community identities, social inequalities, epistemic debates about information, and the correspondence between news and democracy.

We begin this essay with an overview of journalism studies as a field and where digital journalism studies research fits within it as a subfield. We then reassess the application of our six commitments (Carlson et al. 2018) in light of "digital" as a key construct that gives rise to "digital journalism studies." In this exercise, we pay attention to the spatial, temporal, and related boundary characteristics that structure the digital transformation of journalism. We argue that digital technologies – of multimedia, Interactivity, algorithms, automation, and related computational processes and properties – represent transformative actants and actors in mediated ecologies (cf. Lewis and Westlund 2015). Thus, in this essay, we "locate the digital" by declaring "digital journalism studies" a bounded subfield of journalism studies that demands its own approaches and appreciations. Keeping the tag "studies" for this scholarly domain also acknowledges that the multitude of research projects hang together with their broad, common objectives to understand how journalism transforms along with new technologies.

Journalism Studies and Digital Research

As the discipline of (mass) communication has matured during the past century, its development has been marked by the influence of existing theories imported from other domains (such as political science, sociology, feminism, and cultural studies) and also by the developing of theories unique to mass communication (such as agenda-setting, hostile media effect, and cultivation theory). During the past half-century, journalism studies grew out of this hybrid tradition, with roots extending across scholarly bodies and also deep within communication as a discipline. The institutionalization of journalism studies coincides with a need for more conceptual clarity about what it is that the field cares about. As part of this effort at institutionalizing "journalism studies," we outlined some parameters for this emergent field in the 2018 *Journal of Communication* piece:

> Journalism studies examines the realm of informative, public texts involving news and the people, organizations, professions, institutions, and material artifacts and technologies that produce those texts as well as the individuals and multivariate forces shaping their circulation and consumption. Rather than approaching these texts myopically, journalism studies adopts the understanding of news media as part of societal ecosystems in which all actions—and non-actions—have ramifications for other parts of the ecology. … Thus, journalism studies is, in essence, an empirically driven inquiry into understanding and explaining ways in which journalism reifies power structures, social identities, and hierarchies. It focuses on how people construct meaning and situate themselves in the world via journalism as well as how democracy and other political regimes are reinforced (and undermined) through information flows. (Carlson et al. 2018: 9–10)

When we add "digital" to journalism studies for the subfield digital journalism studies, the connotation is naturally one of change. Digital technology affects many journalistic aspects: configurations of people, products, and processes; arrangements of work, labor, and authority; and institutional relationships with politics, economics, and society broadly. It changes social relationships with combinations of audiences/users/citizens/communities as well as official sources, activists, and other voices, in addition to sociotechnical relationships involving machines and automatization. Digital media shift the forms and functions of content, the replicability and spread of information, and the roles of platforms, gatekeepers, distributors, and so forth. All of these changes can be studied at micro, meso, and macro levels – from the smallest newsroom to the largest nation-state. And through these changes, our relationships with time (immediate, historical, future) and with space/place (symbolic, corporeal, physical, virtual, geographic, workspace, etc.) morph in turn. Through digital media, information conveys both the material and the symbolic, and offers journalism home and travel, competition and sanctuary. Transformation comes in the form of algorithms and big data, infographics and computational journalism. It calls up discussion about incivility and fake news as well as bloggers-as-journalists and journalism-as-activism. Through digital media, we can co-opt labor for free; we can make money with no professional credentials; and, we can also lose money, swamped by an overly saturated information market. Through digital media, our questions around journalism ethics take on new and important dimensions. Through digital media, we can feel safe in public spaces and feel disgusted, unnerved, or endangered in what we thought were private places. We are both producer and consumer of information in digital media.

Embedded in these evolutions around our public information flows is the inevitable: transformation. "Transformation" is the changing of one state into another, the altering of sets of norms, and the introduction of new routines. History has long been defined by epochs of transformation that often reflect then-new technologies, such as the printing press or the telegraph. With the internet, World Wide Web, and now ubiquitous technologies of mobile, smart, tablet, wearable, and other devices, we recognize that transformation is endemic to this persistent era of flux. Transformation, in this sense, *is* the "digital," and researchers within digital journalism studies must appreciate the transformation innate in bringing news production, distribution, consumption, manipulation, and sharing from offline or analog worlds into virtual spaces that fundamentally change relationships between journalists and their audiences. But how might this play out in research? We chose the word "transformation" intentionally, shying away from something like "revolutionary" that would dismiss entrenched structures that stay foundational even in digital change. A focus on transformation adjusts temporal and spatial habits of production, distribution, and consumption online while attending to how forces from offline worlds inform these shifts. Many scholars have demonstrated how digital technologies do not upend social structures but solidify hierarchies and reproduce offline trends, including the perpetuation of racism and sexism or the manipulation of publics in the guise of democracy. As a concept undergirding digital media studies, transformation does not equate to the assumption of progress or the shedding of enduring structures. Instead, for the purposes of theory building, the perspective of transformation allows that the essence of a thing being transformed – in this case, journalism – may remain even as transformation opens the possibility for new and/or evolving characteristics to emerge. Thus, neither "evolution" nor "change" go far enough to recognize the metamorphosis that occurs when we move from unidimensional realms to more dynamic spaces. Transformation encourages a research perspective centered on change while also allowing for the maintenance of a status quo.

Digital Journalism Transformation According to Propositions

This notion that "transformation" is the real significance of "digital" highlights research being done at all levels of society and signals the constant need to re-theorize. Now we can apply the six previously articulated scholarly commitments for the field of journalism studies to begin to understand where digital journalism studies manifests. These six propositions are contextual sensitivity, holistic relationality, comparative inclination, normative awareness, embedded communicative power, and methodological pluralism. Each of these offers a way of thinking about what *digital* journalism studies should accomplish. As cultural, political, informational, and other kinds of transformation occur, an application of these six propositions points to the possibilities for new approaches to old questions related to journalism as part of the subfield of digital journalism studies.

Commitment One: Contextual Sensitivity

Journalism studies refuses to accept that journalism can be meaningfully separated from its context, despite journalists' declarations of autonomy. Acknowledging that various social, economic, and political factors continue to affect journalism in whatever form it takes, we wish to draw attention to specific contextual issues encased in the "digital" modifier. Perhaps ironically, much of the technology of digital news falls away in studies of digital journalism. Certainly, studies of production shift to include new tools, and studies of audiences have to account for the myriad ways in which we encounter news. But there are also deeper issues surrounding these tools that an orientation toward the contextual sensitivity of digital journalism studies might unearth. For example, Braun (2015) argues that digital distribution platforms have gone under-examined, despite the fact that "decisions about distribution, whether made by media executives or file sharers, are—in the barest terms—attempts to control who has access to information and culture, and under what conditions" (7). Our ability to wait in line at the grocery store and watch news clips on a smartphone screen involves a largely hidden (and/or ignored or misunderstood) array of sociotechnical actors, long development histories and hiccups, political and economic forces at work, as well as regulations, policies, and protocols. While digital has a tendency to make technology disappear because of its cross-platform ubiquity, an emphasis on contextual sensitivity serves as a reminder that, even in transformation, these actors have power over what news emerges and what it looks like. To this end, contextual sensitivity tempers transformation from fully materializing as it might with no pre-existing context.

Commitment Two: Holistic Relationality

If contextual sensitivity points to the setting in which journalism occurs, holistic relationality reminds us to focus on the relationships that exist in that setting. A digitally specific view of relationality directs our attention to the ways in which transformative technologies influence the networks and associative properties of journalism: for example, vastly expanding opportunities for people to participate in the creation and circulation of public information, opening doors for programmers and technologists to play a greater part in building news products, and complicating boundaries between journalists, citizens, and marketers, as well as publishers and platforms. To build on the above example of getting news in the grocery store, the contextual arrangement of specific tools and tendencies influences how news reaches people at interstitial moments of their virtual every day. A relational view, in turn, gestures to the structural relationships that convey and also compromise journalism in a broader sense: revealing, for instance, how a variety of platforms that were never intended as journalistic venues – Facebook, Twitter, Instagram, YouTube, and more – have become major news gatekeepers (Bell and Owen 2017). In digital journalism studies, then, journalists move from the institutional to the personal, and citizens may connect directly to news sources. This kind of transformation complicates assumed sets of relationships between media and society. Ultimately, the "digital" and any transformative effects need to be continuously interrogated in connection with the many relationships – including those internal and external to the news organization – that constitute journalism (Lewis and Westlund 2015).

Commitment Three: Comparative Inclination

In step with being attuned to context and relationships, digital journalism studies should be wary of overgeneralization, or of failing to compare phenomena across sites, levels of analysis, genres and classes, or geographies. In digital realms, a comparative inclination leads researchers to examine similarities and differences across countries and regions as well as variations across more micro dimensions such as medium and ownership structure. On the one hand, digital transformations of content conceivably flatten and compress geographies and transform the "local" into something less bounded, challenging researchers to continually evaluate the relevance of the usual comparative containers (such as nation-state). On the other hand, digital media have been associated lately with reinforcing nationalism, enabling authoritarian surveillance, and deepening divisions. Thus, befitting its transformative nature, digital media escape easy isolation for comparative research; rather than being a single "level" of analysis in the traditional sense, such study points to variegated outcomes occurring as digital code and culture are enacted differently across time and space. For example, a focus on transformation related to Facebook can highlight how the platform's evolving role as a social, cultural, and political resource differs in respective countries and situations by comparing the opportunities for subversion and/or re-entrenchment. Or, when analyzing relative trust among citizens, it is important not only to think about different media platforms and their transformative nature but also how transnational contexts might influence those attitudes about virtual life, as Elvestad, Phillips, and Feuerstein (2017) found in their multi-method study of news audiences in Israel, Norway, and the United Kingdom. Finally, it should be noted that the kinds of transformations that occur will vary depending on different cultural, economic, political, and other forces.

Commitment Four: Normative Awareness

A norm, once it achieves its normative status, disappears into a state of acceptance. It becomes a shortcut that both dictates and legitimates conduct. For digital journalism studies scholars, we propose thinking of norms not as independent precepts, but rather as ideas promoted (or contested) by various agents – many of them players in the world of content production – according to a range of motivations and from a variety of institutional positions that are facilitated by digital tools and platforms and take shape in virtual places. Being circumspect about any dogmatic claims, digital journalism studies scholars with a normative awareness can expose the assumptions that develop around journalism and can also interrogate any transformative suppositions. Furthermore, rather than being static determinants, norms are continuously enacted and constantly morph. From this starting point, what makes digital journalism studies particularly interesting is how it invites variation within its transformation. As an example of digital journalism studies research in this area, Young and Callison (2017) examine a data journalism startup in Canada wrestling with core questions surrounding how journalism can contribute to ongoing truth and reconciliation practices relating to the historical mistreatment of the country's indigenous population. These journalists struggled with how to develop news work that would break from the colonialist legacy of Canadian news to develop its own orientation. The technology afforded space to experiment with content that would markedly deviate from traditional news, but the journalists also found themselves constantly grappling with pre-existing notions of what constitutes news and how to support themselves as an organization. Such studies reveal the generative nature of digital news in providing for new possibilities that differ not merely at the level of content, but more fundamentally in questioning normative and epistemological assumptions that have been taken-for-granted in journalism. Digital journalism studies should remain attuned to how journalistic norms become objects of debate and experimentation and, in the process, transform into new habits and routines.

Commitment Five: Embedded Communicative Power

In the *Journal of Communication* article, we suggested that journalism studies researchers adopt a critical perspective toward the profession that continually probes how information is reported and produced, and whose voices get heard in that flow. Beyond what we can and cannot do with expanded powers is a need to appreciate how digital media are transforming *how we think* and *who we are* in a more fundamental sense. For example, the ability to publish en masse affects an individual producer's "journalistic capital" and signals dramatic shifts in "access to resources" and "material security," as Örnebring et al. (2018) have argued. The model they outline reflects a Bourdieuian state of production and distribution governed by power structures and actor positionality in addition to the capability to amplify voices in the information stream. In this sense, a continuum of production exists, from *New York Times* reporters with high resources and high journalistic capital to a lone, out-of-work reporter who has low resource capital but high journalistic capital, to an unknown blogger lacking money and connections. This kind of theorizing around the transformation of capital embeds into its understanding a nuanced version of power dynamics as they play out in information production in a digital era. Such digitized transformations often connote a flattening of media space because of the wide accessibility of the technology, but, in reality, hierarchies persist because cultural power is deeply ingrained. As such, the hopes of digital fixes for entrenched social problems can fail. Paying attention to embedded communicative power as we study these transformations allows for an exposing of the policymaking and other kinds of continuity that also inevitably endure in the move from offline to online and vice versa.

Commitment Six: Methodological Pluralism

A multi-dimensional, multi-methodological approach is a key proposition when outlining the parameters of transformation in digital spaces. The spirit of methodological pluralism asks the researcher to position herself temporally (e.g., recognizing her current time period in relation to context, to be attuned to temporal fluctuations present in old links, for example) as well as spatially (e.g., making sure she has the necessary permissions for online observations, understanding virtual and unseen work, being hyper-aware of any bias her corporeal presence might bring, etc.; Robinson and Metzler 2016). Multiple methods can best appreciate digital aspects of news content, production, distribution, and consumption as part of interrelated flows of information – every bit of which is subject to the associative networks of the institutions, organizations, and individuals that make up the overall ecology of the media landscape. Multifarious approaches will have better precision in considering digital units of analysis (such as posts or tweets) where in one context the sample yields one set of findings and in another something else entirely. Reinforcing mechanisms such as "member checks" or the triangulation of techniques can aid in reliability as well. We point to how Ottovordemgentschenfelde (2017) explores digital journalists' constructed identities by looking not only at how and what they tweet, but also at their entire digital presence., Anderson (2018) writes, "We must take both the variety of journalistic objects of evidence and their cultural, political, organizational, and social embeddedness seriously" (p. 195). He establishes his methodological approach using documents, interviews, and observation to understand the intersectional relationships between computational journalism, politics, social science and what is meant by "fact" and "truth." Anderson's book highlights how a multi-method approach can parse out the varying degrees of transformation present in a new digital journalism studies phenomenon such as data reporting.

Conclusion

In journalism studies, research takes place within news ecosystems comprising relationships between actors and actants where power forces dictate production, distribution, and consumption and where meaning is constructed contextually and ritually. Locating the "digital" in journalism studies for the emergent subfield of digital journalism studies stresses the way technologies are brandished and manipulated in the name of information exchange within these structures. With each app, algorithm, ping, post, tweet, link, emoji, share, mashup, and "friend" or "follower," voices can be amplified through digitized networks yet still constrained by online and offline hierarchies. In this essay, we have theorized *transformation* as the inevitable outcome when new technologies enter media ecologies. In transformation, infrastructural relationships change, adapt, and sometimes become more entrenched at macro, meso, and micro levels of society. Digital journalism studies scholars exploring transformations (note the emphasized plural), ranging from time and space contexts to emergent norms to shifting power dynamics, should remain aware of the commitments we have summarized. In appreciating the socio-cultural, spatial-temporal environment of digital journalism objects and artifacts, actors and processes, we understand their significant transformative properties holistically in terms of what they mean for the professions as well as for politics, economics, culture, society, and ourselves.

Acknowledgments

We thank the three anonymous reviewers and the editors for their constructive feedback and willingness to publish the continuation of this conversation around journalism studies. In addition, we appreciate the comments of Dan Berkowitz as they embarked on this venture.

Disclosure statement

No potential conflict of interest was reported by the authors.

Note

1. Beyond the scope of this essay but nevertheless worth noting here is the fact that digital media, by virtue of their cloud computing and internet architecture, have a deeply *physical* dimension – as evident, for example, in massive server farms that account for a growing share of carbon emissions because of their electricity use.

ORCID

Seth C. Lewis http://orcid.org/0000-0001-7498-0599
Matt Carlson http://orcid.org/0000-0001-5674-5595

References

Anderson, C. W. 2018. *Apostles of Certainty: Data Journalism and the Politics of Doubt*. Oxford: Oxford University Press.

Bell, Emily, and Taylor Owen. 2017. "The Platform Press: How Silicon Valley Reengineered Journalism." *Tow Center for Digital Journalism Report, March 29. Columbia Journalism Review.* https://www.cjr.org/tow_center_reports/platform-press-how-silicon-valley-reengineered-journalism.php/

Braun, Joshua. A. 2015. *This Program is Brought to you by … : Distributing Television News Online.* New Haven, CT: Yale University Press.

Carlson, Matt, and Sue Robinson, Seth C. Lewis, and Daniel A. Berkowitz. 2018. "Journalism Studies and its Core Commitments: The Making of a Communication Field." *The Journal of Communication* 68 (1): 6–25.

Elvestad, Eiri, and Angela Phillips, and Mira Feuerstein. 2017. "Can Trust in Traditional News Media Explain Cross-National Differences in News Exposure of Young People Online?" *Digital Journalism* 6 (2): 215–235.

Hermida, Alfred. 2010. "Twittering the News: The Emergence of Ambient Journalism." *Journalism Practice* 4 (3): 297–308.

Lewis, Seth C., and Oscar Westlund. 2015. "Actors, Actants, Audiences, and Activities in Cross-media News Work: A Matrix and a Research Agenda." *Digital Journalism* 3 (1): 19–37.

Örnebring, Henrik, and Michael Karlsson, Karin Fast, and Johan Lindell. 2018. "The Space of Journalistic Work: A Theoretical Model." *Communication Theory* 28 (4): 403–423. doi:10.1093/ct/qty006

Ottovordemgentschenfelde, Sylvia. 2017. "'Organizational, Professional, Personal': An Exploratory Study of Political Journalists and Their Hybrid Brand on Twitter." *Journalism* 18 (1): 64–80.

Peters, Benjamin. 2016. "Digital." In *Digital Keywords: A Vocabulary of Information Society and Culture*, edited by B. Peters, 93–108. Princeton, NJ: Princeton University Press.

Robinson, Sue and Meredith Metzler. 2016. "Ethnography in Digital Newsrooms." In *The SAGE Handbook of Digital Journalism*, edited by Tamara Witschge, C. W. Anderson, David Domingo, and Alfred Hermida. London: Sage.

Singer, Jane B. 2018. "Transmission Creep: Media Effects Theories and Journalism Studies in a Digital Era." *Journalism Studies* 19 (2): 209–226.

Steensen, Steen, and Laura Ahva. 2015. "Theories of Journalism in a Digital Age." *Digital Journalism* 3 (1): 1–18, Doi:10.1080/21670811.2014.927984.

Young, Mary Lynn, and Candis Callison. 2017. "When Gender, Colonialism, and Technology Matter in a Journalism Startup." *Journalism.* doi:10.1177/1464884917743390

Digital Journalism: Defined, Refined, or Re-defined

Andrew Duffy and Peng Hwa Ang

ABSTRACT

Observing the limitations driven by a certain path-dependency in most scholarship on digital journalism, we argue for favouring a direction that privileges "digital" over "journalism". Rather than seeing it as a digital iteration of journalistic principles, as has been a persistent theme in academia to date, it would see consider journalism as an embodiment of digital principles, one of the many domains of social life which is increasingly restructured around digital technologies. Digitisation sets the agenda for journalism to follow, rather than journalism setting the agenda for its digital incarnation to live up to—or not. Such an approach is a continuation of existing but limited scholarship which could open up new paths and expand current avenues of research, and reflects an emerging paradigm where digitisation is the dominant partner.

CONCEPT DEFINITION: Digital Journalism

Gone Digital

It is hard to disentangle journalism from digital technology. Considering print journalism, for example, the entire process from finding a source to recording an interview, to the pecking and tapping on a smartphone or tablet or laptop, to the writing, editing and sub-editing, to the layout, printing and distribution is more than likely to involve digitisation. Only physical, foldable newsprint remains resolutely analogue. Digitisation has brought speed, innovation, complexity, sociality, connectivity, storability, searchability, and above all flexibility to journalism. Outside the newsroom, meanwhile, the computing power to distribute information digitally is now available cheaply to the public, who can write, post, share and comment to large audiences bypassing traditional media channels. This access to computing power among the "digital haves" has changed the face of the news media industry and its associated scholarship. We argue, then, that an updated definition of the term "digital journalism" should begin not with "journalism" but instead with "digital". In this conceptualisation, digital journalism is not journalism that is transformed by being digital; it is digitisation as it is embodied in journalism.

A starting point for a definition of digitisation is "the way many domains of social life are restructured around digital communication and media infrastructures" (Brennan and Kreiss 2016, 385). By way of illustration of some of these domains, digitisation impacts on journalism's social affordances as people share news stories via social media, for instance. It impacts on the cultural domain as the internet distributes news beyond national boundaries and allows for a related flow of information and opinions around those stories that crosses borders and cultures. Its professional dimension includes the fresh possibilities presented by user-generated content and increased awareness of audiences based on web analytics. Digitisation today, however, goes beyond Brennan and Kreiss's definition centring it on social life, opening up new legal vistas in the domain of privacy, with emerging data protection legislation on the one hand and evolving notions of personal privacy online on the other hand. It drives new assessments of transparency in an era of big data gathered and applied by corporations and governments, as well as fake news (e.g., Tandoc, Lim, and Ling 2017). While journalism as the "first draft of history" has traditionally represented the fixity of fact, in its digitised incarnation it now represents the fluidity of flow.

Following the "4Vs" model of big data, digitisation has changed the volume of news the public receives, the velocity with which it is delivered, the variety of sources it comes from, and the audience's assessment of its veracity. Together, they add to the uncertainty which surrounds news journalism. One impact of this digitally engendered uncertainty has been both to drive readers and viewers away from news as a whole as untrustworthy; or paradoxically to drive them back towards reputable, credible, traditional news brands. Either way, digitisation leads and journalism follows.

Looking Backwards to Move Forwards

Such an approach preferring digitisation over journalism as a baseline would broaden and extend a trail that several scholars have already blazed, such as Wahl-Jorgensen's essay arguing against the "newsroom-centricity" of journalistic research which has favoured study of its routinised elements over its innovative aspects (2009). Hermida (2010), meanwhile, has explored "ambient journalisms" as a phenomenon driven by digital technologies and their widespread adoption into everyday life in many societies. This essay builds on studies by them and similar scholars to offer a refined redefinition of what digital journalism *is*.

An editorial in the first issue of this journal sketches out the perimeter as "digital technologies for the practice and study of journalism" (Franklin 2013, 1), setting the tone by observing the fundamental changes in journalism wrought by digitisation. Franklin extrapolates from there to the implications for the "economic, social, political and cultural life of communities and nations". Early on, therefore, this journal established a series of agendas which may have constrained what is of interest. One might critique the journal's gaze as having a wide reach, but consequently lacking a focus. And while this offers invaluable guidelines for submission, it appears to have led to a particular outlook towards digital innovation (Wahl-Jorgensen 2017).

To continue moving scholarship on digital journalism forward, therefore, we return to the starting point by assessing the 1,675 keywords and key terms for the 277 original research articles published in *Digital Journalism* between its launch in 2013 and issue 6.5 in mid-2018. This allows us to see how the map has been drawn thus far with a view to refining it. Keywords are of interest not because they represent what has appeared in the journal but because they appeal to what scholars anticipate will be of interest to future generations.

Digital Journalism's emphasis on *journalism/journalists* is expected and evident, appearing 312 times among keywords, while *digitised/digital* (60 keywords) is most often of significance as it relates to journalism rather than vice versa. Digital technology is often analysed as it fits into existing newsworker patterns of sourcing, verification and breaking news (e.g., Verweij and van Noort 2014). *Mobility* (16) concerns news production and MOJOs more than as a means for news to fit into an audience's mobile digital lives. *Blogs* (9) are either assessed in terms of their linking norms to professional journalists and institutions, or refer to journalists' live blogging rather than non-journalistic bloggers contributing to the news. At the lower end of the scale are *robots* (11) and *drones* (9), while *government* and *law* each appear three times and *truth* only once.

As evidence of the limitations caused by this "newsroom-first" approach, one persistent theme in *Digital Journalism* has been that digitisation brings opportunities to journalism that have not been realised. For example, Borger et al. (2013) find that scholars express disappointment at the passivity of users and journalists. Similarly, the shock of encountering real rather than imaginary readers causes discomfort to newsworkers who then compromise on quality to please readers with the result that both end up disappointed (Aitamurto 2013). Similarly, articles primarily consider how journalists use social media to source, verify and report—how they use it to accomplish established journalistic tasks (e.g., Thurman 2018). Caple (2014) reports that newsrooms using user-generated content photography need to place more emphasis on editing and packaging to ensure quality for readers. New media are assessed according to old media norms: Price (2017) asks of a new publication "Can *The Ferret* be a watchdog?" The use of Twitter to brand journalists is similarly analysed according to journalistic norms (Molyneux and Holton 2015), while Hedman (2015) finds that tweeting journalists do not depart from core newsroom values. Reader comments are also made to fit in with journalistic routines and values (Carlson 2015; Wolfgang 2018).

The clearest evidence of journalism's dominant place in *Digital Journalism* (and we extend this beyond the journal itself to include most current scholarly interpretations of the subject) is therefore the recurring theme of boundary work. Domingo and Le Cam (2014) note that journalists maintain a hegemonic position over narrative by dismissing alternative voices and preferring institutional ones. Loosen (2014), in looking at how boundaries blur in journalism, questions whether the new term "de-boundedness" is just a catch-all term for the changes being faced by the industry. This blurring of boundaries shapes journalists and journalism, introducing new questions such as who decides who is to be the audience? Journalism's boundaries now encompass audiences, algorithms and analytics. Editors consider page views and viewing time to attribute value to news stories while, at another level of analysis, every audience ultimately decides what they consider is valued as news by paying or not. In the digital space, the audience has a larger say, too, and news consumers have unintentionally and indirectly become "news" producers through easier access to digital content creation and distribution technologies.

Consider one little-discussed embodiment of audience-turned-reporter that is shifting these boundaries: online vigilantism. The scenario for online vigilantism making the news begins with traditional media ignoring or overlooking offending behaviour, for whatever reason. Non-journalistic digital media then acts: first, netizens go online to seek out digital information to uncover further incriminating details about the aberrant person; they publish it digitally with a view to naming and shaming, and perhaps harassment. Only at this stage, because of the virality of the content as it is shared through digital social networks, is it picked up by traditional journalists to become news. In some countries, notably China, such online vigilantism has led to officials being convicted of corruption and jailed. Such convictions and subsequent press coverage lend credence to online vigilantism; people start to ask, what is so wrong with breaches of privacy if it results in the convictions of corrupt officials? The capabilities of citizens and their relationship with traditional news media has been changed.

Yet in scholarly studies, audiences are more often considered insofar as their perceptions of journalism conform to or depart from newsworkers norms (e.g., Schmidt and Loosen 2015). Many news organisations had existed for decades with only a rudimentary and indirect understanding of who their audience was. Now, any focus on consumers has been forced upon news organisations by financial pressures. Yet, while laudable, any attempts to target the reader pose increasingly urgent questions over the extent to which the readers' interests should be catered to—questions which could be glossed over in the days before digitisation delivered such precise knowledge of who they are and what they like.

The most significant change wrought by digitisation as a factor in journalism is this renegotiation of boundaries. Lines blur between producer and consumer, between gatekeeper and audience, between catering to the reader and letting the reader choose, between the privacy of those reading and those written about, leading to fundamental questions being asked again. What is the main aim of journalism? For political ends? For entertainment? Or to evoke emotions? What makes people click? Interest? Anger? Fake news? Is there a need to be balanced? If so, should each individual media outlet itself be balanced so that a reader receiving news from only that one organisation would have a reasonably nuanced view of the world? Or would it suffice if the eco-system as a whole was balanced? Digitisation promises far greater choice; but that does not oblige it to deliver on that promise.

Other fundamental questions being asked include that of privacy, long a core issue for journalism, making digitisation in journalism a matter for policymakers as much as for media organisations. Digital journalism is under greater responsibility to address privacy not as a legal obligation such as the GDPR (General Data Protection Regulation) but as an ethical one. It is easier to invade privacy in a digital environment; as the incidents in China show, it may be easier to hold public officials accountable through digital journalism. But what of the average citizen? The GDPR can protect the individual's personal data, information that by itself can identify the individual, typically for purposes of marketing or surveillance. But such privacy rules cannot guard against the release of secrets, which is one interest of journalism.

Privileging the digital therefore also means that journalists need to be more self-reflective, relying more on ethics than the law, because too much of the definition of privacy and its intrusion is context-sensitive (Loosen 2011). Wider policies for digital media as a whole thereby impact on the boundaries of what is and what is not permissible for journalism.

Privilege the Digital

We do not say that all articles in *Digital Journalism* have privileged journalism, and there are several which examine how digital values are manifested in journalistic practice, such as one article which asks what makes headlines effective to drive click-through (Kuiken et al. 2017). Sites such as Buzzfeed, alongside traditional legacy newsrooms, use search-engine optimisation to drive click-through; but while mainstream press sought to apply SEO to their journalism, Buzzfeed emerged *from* the principles of SEO and created a novel form of journalism to reflect the new digital paradigm. Another article moves news away from being a product and imagines it as a service to citizens, shifting the focus away from the producers and towards the consumers which allows for a novel iteration of what journalism is in the digital era (Artwick 2013). Doherty (2014), meanwhile, circumvents the text-orientation and linearity of legacy news journalism to examine how the digital space affords the possibility of hypertext as a new form of narrativity. Likewise, data visualisation is seen as a sufficiently novel area for new technology to set the agenda in evolving new forms of narrative (Smit, de Haan, and Bujis 2014); yet Dick (2014) still finds that journalistic and organisational norms define news infographic production. Schifferes et al. (2014), meanwhile, keep journalism in the background by asking what kind of technology would be best for surfing social media to find stories suitable for an audience. Wikileaks—a crisis (or opportunity) made possible by digitisation—might be visualised as forcing journalism to confront its own definitional crisis, emerging legal issues, and the complexities of global information flows; that is, to consider how journalism can follow where digitisation leads (Lynch 2013).

The challenge for any attempt to define the term "digital journalism" is that it will cleave too closely to the first or the second word in the couple. Given the task of defining the boundaries, therefore, we set out instead to refine them. Our suggestion is that the scholarly community should approach digital journalism by privileging the digital.

> We therefore define digital journalism as the way in which journalism embodies the philosophies, norms, practices, values and attitudes of digitisation as they relate to society. These include the efficiency of control, storage, retrieval, accessibility and transmission of data; inclusivity, interactivity and collaboration in the propagation of information and opinion; flexibility and innovation in presenting news stories; and state, institutional and individual ownership of data and its implications for privacy and transparency.

Each of these philosophies, practices, values and attitudes can be through journalism, changing some aspects from the analogue era and maintaining others. Rather than being concerned with how digitisation impacts on journalism, the question becomes how digitisation finds an incarnation in journalism. This involves losing the normative accretions surrounding journalism and starting from the principles of digit-isation as articulated through the news media. It requires a continued shift of focus away from legacy news production and how digitisation is being worked into the newsroom, to consider instead how digitisation is a feature of society and how jour-nalism subsequently articulates or informs that. This will allow some established friends into the room: digitisation opens the doors for under-represented communities to speak, for citizens to be heard, for specialist groups to connect, for publics to rally. It introduces novel forms of multimedia creativity, delivering new narrative forms. It makes information searchable, so that it can be repurposed, redirected and revitalised, or misrepresented, degraded and corrupted. Such an approach is not a departure from the existing remit of the journal, of course. Lewis and Westlund have already observed the value in framing the study of digital journalism in terms of a collabor-ation of human actors and technological actants (2015), while Hermida (2013) has also argued for introducing new paradigms and breaking away from the old. Specifically, for example, focusing on an affordance of digitisation—ease of circulation—rather than on the texts that are circulated (Bødker 2015). We argue only for greater emphasis on this path rather than a complete change in direction.

Finally, there are also practical—and awkwardly commercial—reasons to consider digitisation as a dominant partner rather than a qualifier. Legacy journalism's busi-ness model is broken; new ideas are needed from digitisation. It is incumbent on journalism to pursue the digital, then. This will drive change, loss and cost, growth, experimentation and innovation. Each of these will be driven by the cowboy ways of digitisation rather than being corralled, tamed and ridden by journalism. Several authors have looked into digital journalism's economic imperative, considering com-mercial crossovers between editorial and business (e.g., Drew and Thomas 2018) or where it impacts on audience perception of legacy and online news publishers (Amazeen and Muddiman 2018), or paywalls as a new option—and how unsuccessful they have been in replacing the funding from advertisers (Myllylahti 2014; Pickard and Williams 2014).

We argue therefore that the original parameters for *Digital Journalism* would benefit from loosening. Set tight, the journal's view has predominantly (although not invariably) been from *within* the newsroom. Indeed, one reason digital innov-ation in journalism has received a chilly welcome in newsroom and news scholar-ship alike is that it starts from the perspective of journalism—where the question is "what is being changed?"—rather than of digitisation—where the question becomes "what can we do?" Starting from journalism has created path-dependency in the face of innovation. Better for "journalism" to qualify "digitisation" so that the digital is embodied in journalism and its relationship with society. Most importantly, these changes are also enacted in response to the need for journalism's survival by evolving as a subsidiary to the successfully—and often profitably—developing digital ecosystem.

Disclosure Statement

No potential conflict of interests was reported by the authors.

References

Aitamurto, Tanja. 2013. "New Forms of Collaborative Innovation and Production on the Internet: An Interdisciplinary Perspective." *Digital Journalism* 1 (2): 291–292.

Amazeen, Michelle A., and Ashley R. Muddiman. 2018. "Saving Media or Trading on Trust? The Effects of Native Advertising on Audience Perceptions of Legacy and Online News Publishers." *Digital Journalism* 6 (2): 176–195.

Artwick, Claudette G. 2013. "Reporters on Twitter: Product or Service?" *Digital Journalism* 1 (2): 212–228.

Bødker, Henrik. 2015. "Journalism as Cultures of Circulation." *Digital Journalism* 3 (1): 101–115.

Borger, Merel, Anita van Hoof, Irene Costera Meijer and José Sanders. 2013. "Constructing Participatory Journalism as a Scholarly Object: A Genealogical Analysis." *Digital Journalism* 1 (1): 117–113.

Brennan, J Scott, and Daniel Kreiss. 2016. "Digitalization". In *The International Encyclopedia of Communication Theory and Philosophy*, edited by Klaus Bruhn Jensen and Robert Craig, Hoboken, NJ: Wiley Online Library.

Caple, Helen. 2014. "Anyone Can Take a Photo, But: Is There Space for the Professional Photographer in the 21st-Century Newsroom?" *Digital Journalism* 2 (3): 355–365.

Carlson, Matt. 2015. "The Robotic Reporter: Automated Journalism and the Redefinition of Labor, Compositional Forms, and Journalistic Authority." *Digital Journalism* 3 (3): 416–443.

Dick, Murray. 2014. "Interactive Infographics and News Values." *Digital Journalism* 2 (4): 490–506.

Doherty, Skye. 2014. "Hypertext and Journalism: Paths for Future Research." *Digital Journalism* 2 (2): 124–139.

Domingo, David, and Florence Le Cam. 2014. "Journalism In Dispersion: Exploring the Blurring Boundaries of Newsmaking Through a Controversy." *Digital Journalism* 2 (3): 310–321.

Drew, Kevin K., and Ryan J. Thomas. 2018. "From Separation to Collaboration: Perspectives on Editorial-Business Collaboration at United States News Organizations." *Digital Journalism* 6 (2): 196–215.

Franklin, Bob. 2013. "Editorial." *Digital Journalism* 1(1): 1–5.

Hermida, Alfred. 2010. "Twittering the News: The Emergence of Ambient Journalism." *Journalism Practice* 4 (3): 297–308.

Hermida, Alfred. 2013. "#Journalism: Reconfiguring Journalism Research About Twitter, One Tweet at a Time." *Digital Journalism* 1 (3): 295–313.

Kuiken, Jeffrey, Anne Schuth, Martijn Spitters and Maarten Marx. 2017. "Effective Headlines of Newspaper Articles in a Digital Environment." *Digital Journalism* 5 (10): 1300–1314.

Lewis, Seth C. and Oscar Westlund. 2015. "Big Data and Journalism: Epistemology, Expertise, Economics, and Ethics." *Digital Journalism* 3 (3): 447–466.

Loosen, Weibke. 2011. "Online Privacy as a News Factor in Journalism." In *Privacy Online: Perspectives on Privacy and Self-Disclosure in the Social Web, edited by* S. Trepte and L. Reinecke, 205–218. Berlin: Springer-Verlag.

Loosen, Wiebke. 2014. "The Notion of the 'Blurring Boundaries': Journalism as a (De-) Differentiated Phenomenon." *Digital Journalism* 3 (1): 68–84.

Lynch, Lisa. 2013. "Wikileaks After Megaleaks: The Organization's Impact on Journalism and Journalism Studies." *Digital Journalism* 1 (3): 314–333.

Molyneux, Logan, and Avery Holton. 2015. "Branding (Health) Journalism: Perceptions, Practices and Emerging Norms." *Digital Journalism* 3 (2): 225–242.

Myllylahti, Merja. 2014. "Newspaper Paywalls—the Hype and the Reality: A Study of How Paid News Content Impacts on Media Corporation Revenues." *Digital Journalism* 2 (2): 179–194.

Pickard, Victor, and Alex T. Williams. 2014. "Salvation Or Folly? The Promises and Perils of Digital Paywalls." *Digital Journalism* 2 (2): 195–213.

Price, John. 2017. "Can The Ferret be a Watchdog? Understanding the Launch, Growth and Prospects of a Digital, Investigative Journalism Set-Up." *Digital Journalism* 5 (10): 1336–1350.

Schifferes, Steve, Nic Newman, Neil Thurman, David Corney, Ayse Göker and Carlos Martin. 2014. "Identifying and Verifying News through Social Media: Developing a User-Centred Tool for Professional Journalists." *Digital Journalism* 2 (3): 406–418.

Schmidt, Jan-Hinrik, and Wiebke Loosen. 2015. "Both Sides of the Story: Accessing Audience Participation Through the Concept of Inclusion Distance." *Digital Journalism* 3 (2): 259–278.

Smit, Gerard, Yael de Haan and Laura Buijs. 2014. "Visualizing News: Make it Work." *Digital Journalism* 2 (3): 344–354.

Tandoc, Edson, Zheng Wei Lim, and Richard Ling. 2017. "Defining 'Fake News': A Typology of Scholarly Definitions." *Digital Journalism* 6 (2): 137–153.

Thurman, Neil. 2018. "Social Media, Surveillance, and News Work: On the Apps Promising Journalists a 'Crystal Ball.'" *Digital Journalism* 6 (1): 76–97.

Verweij, Peter, and Elvira van Noort. 2014. "Journalists' Twitter Networks, Public Debates and Relationships in South Africa." *Digital Journalism* 2 (1): 98–114.

Wahl-Jorgensen, Karin. 2009. "News Production, Ethnography, and Power: On the Challenges of Newsroom-Centricity." In *The Anthropology of News and Journalism: Global Perspectives*, edited by S. Elizabeth Bird, 21–35. Bloomington: Indiana University Press.

Wahl-Jorgensen, Karin. 2017. "A Manifesto for Failure in Digital Journalism." In *Remaking the News: Essays on the Future of Journalism Scholarship in the Digital Era*, edited by Pablo Bczkowski, and C. W. Anderson, 251–266. Cambridge, MA: MIT Press.

Wolfgang, J. David. 2018. "Cleaning up the 'Fetid Swamp' Examining How Journalists Construct Policies and Practices for Moderating Comments." *Digital Journalism* 6 (1): 21–40.

Navigating the Scholarly Terrain: Introducing the Digital Journalism Studies Compass

Scott A. Eldridge II ⓘ, Kristy Hess ⓘ, Edson C. Tandoc, Jr. ⓘ and Oscar Westlund ⓘ

ABSTRACT
This article by the *Digital Journalism* Editorial Team surfaces with the explicit ambition to reassess the field of *Digital Journalism Studies* and map a future editorial agenda for *Digital Journalism*. The article dissects two important and closely interrelated questions: *"What is 'digital journalism'?"*, and *"What is 'digital journalism studies'?"* Building on the commissioned conceptual articles and the review article also published in this issue, we define *Digital Journalism Studies* as a field which should strive to critically explore, document, and explain the interplay of digital and journalism, continuity and change, and further focus, conceptualize, and theorize tensions, configurations, power imbalances, and the debates these continue to raise for digital journalism and its futures. We also present a useful heuristic device—the Digital Journalism Studies Compass—anchored around *digital* and *journalism*, and *continuity* and *change*, as a guide for discussing the direction of the growing field and this journal.

Introduction

In this article we grapple with core questions at the heart of this journal: what is digital journalism, and what is digital journalism studies? Building on the foundation outlined by founding editor-in-chief Bob Franklin in launching this journal, we begin by dissecting these two important and closely interrelated questions through discussions of debates and definitions in previous literature (Part I). Second, we establish the context for our examination and synthesize the key arguments and threads of inquiry from the conceptual and review article(s) we have presented in this special issue. In discussing these, we have developed a table presenting an overview of the concise definitions offered by all contributors to the special issue, adding our own discussion of the larger field of study (Part II). Third, and on the basis of these discussions, we turn towards generating anchor points for the field of *Digital Journalism Studies*, a process that is aided by what we call the *Digital Journalism Studies Compass* (DJS Compass). This compass allows us to navigate the geographies of a dynamic field, and embraces the continuums between *digital* and *journalism*, and between *continuity* and *change*, reflected in digital journalism research and the contributions being made (Part III).

Our generation of a metaphorical DJS Compass is part of an effort to highlight what distinguishes digital journalism studies, and digital journalism as its core priority, from work in journalism studies. Why a compass? A compass provides navigators with clear direction when conditions are overcast—a useful metaphor for those studying the news during this period of intense digitization and disruption. A compass has no cultural bias—it has been used for divination as early as the Chinese Han Dynasty and was integral to the Age of Discovery, a period where extensive overseas exploration from Europe marked the beginning of globalization. In our thinking through this metaphor, and considering Digital Journalism Studies as a field as it has taken shape, we envisage the compass as an orienteering tool reflective not only of the ways the field has come into being, but of the different ways we, as an editorial team, consider the field from our own orientations—thinking through these ideas while we are situated in the East, South, North, and West.

Let us begin by interacting with two questions at the core of this effort, and this issue of *Digital Journalism*: "what is 'digital journalism'?", and "what is 'digital journalism studies'?". In doing so, we show here that these are not questions with isolated responses; rather, answering each helps better inform responses to the other.

Revisiting the burgeoning line of research into *Digital Journalism* (Part I)

To examine these questions, it is useful to first look back to the emergence of scholarly work making sense of the ways the increasingly accessible Web was opening doors to new ways of doing journalism online. At the outset of this century, this was first embraced in groundbreaking work by Singer (2003), Boczkowski (2004), Deuze (2005), Allan (2006), Robinson (2006), among others. These early studies on journalism's transitions to the Web, and the integration of new technologies into familiar routines, identified a set of debates and discussions which have served as rocks on a cairn, incrementally building towards establishing a body of research into digital journalism; or, put differently, looking back from our current vantage point, scholars have amassed a notable body of work in the first two decades of research into the shifting nature of journalism following the emergence of the Web, which better allows us to understand the path this field has taken in its development. Further, the work in the first decades of research in this field offered guiding insights into how a new domain of journalism was emerging, how it was developing, and how quickly it was progressing.

Subsequent large edited collections took these into further consideration and presented a more coherent narrative of a field coming into shape. Key debates were brought together by Witschge, Anderson, Domingo, and Hermida (2016), Franklin and Eldridge (2017), and Eldridge and Franklin (2019), alongside journals, including this one and *Journalism Studies* and *Journalism Practice* before it. Through these collections, scholars sought to grasp how digital technologies emerged and how journalism embraced them with an emphasis on the "fundamental changes in the ways that journalism is produced, engaged with, and critically understood" (Eldridge and Franklin 2019: 1). At the core of these efforts was a recognition that "digital journalism" was not merely a modified description of journalism, but a way of seeing journalism in fundamentally new ways (Figure 1).

Yet confronting the fundamental novelty of digital journalism has also required scholars to recognize that studying digital journalism involves "embracing the ambiguity, unease, and uncertainty of the field" (Witschge et al. 2016: 1). As it has wrestled with journalistic legacies, and digital unknowns, the tenor of research constituting Digital Journalism Studies was established, including in special issues of this journal devoted to its theories (Steensen and Ahva 2015) and methods (Karlsson and Sjøvaag 2016). In broad strokes, this has included work which both hearkens back to a long history of journalism research and the normative, theoretical, and empirical territory journalism studies has staked out, while also setting out to chart a discrete set of terminological reference points unique to the contemporary era. On one level, this continues to define digital journalism research, which rests somewhere between acknowledging continuity, while nevertheless making clear that *something* has changed. Such a bifurcated set of priorities has led to fruitful questions being asked— Was this change altogether, or rather evolutionary? Were the forms of digital journalism a response to digital technologies and how do we address the diverse facets of dependence of journalism on digital technologies, as tools and systems, within a socio-technical environment (Lewis and Westlund 2015)? Where do new forms of digital journalism also point our gaze towards other societal shifts? How much is "digital journalism" still a discrete phenomenon and, if so, how does it draw distinction from "journalism"?

Onward, ever onward, both digital journalism and the study of it has continued to develop, and each soon came to be reflected not only in the advancement of technologies into journalism, but in transforming distinctions between those "formerly known as audiences" and journalists (Bruns 2005; Rosen 2006), and the tensions that came with this shift (Lewis 2012). In time, critical scholarship began to emerge, confronting initial conclusions that the Web was an unbridled space for journalism, and upending the optimism that accompanied such views (Curran, Fenton, and Freedman 2012). A flurry of work reconceptualizing foundational concepts to accommodate digital journalism also followed, marking a shift from the industrial approaches of the twentieth century and a revisiting of journalism's role as a public good (Peters and Broersma 2013), while also pushing through new definitions and boundaries around the field of journalism itself (Belair-Gagnon and Holton 2018; Carlson and Lewis 2015; Eldridge 2018; Lewis 2019). Such work offers specific avenues through which scholars can navigate the interplays between "the digital" and "the journalism", and assess what has changed and what nevertheless remains the same.

Of course, we should not be quick to assume that change equals progress. Caught in the melee of advancing technologies and their implications for the hitherto industry of journalism, further challenges have emerged including, most recently, confrontations to our understanding of journalism as malevolent actors spread something other-than-news under the guise of journalism (Waisbord 2018, c.f. Tandoc, Ling, and Lim 2018), as audiences struggle to scrutinize and verify information as they too navigate change (Tandoc *et al.* 2018), and as advertisers seize on "fake news" as a revenue stream (Braun and Eklund 2019). The fact that content that disrupts journalism's allegiance with truth-telling succeeds creates incipient challenges as does the success of third-party digital platforms such as Facebook, where distribution and exposure are beyond the control of newsrooms, and fail to provide significant revenue streams for "real" news media (Myllylahti 2018).

Further critical questions have also emerged as media platforms beyond journalism's institutional control begin to come into our fields of view—social media as but one example. During the past decades there has also been tremendous research activity into the intersection of journalism and social media (cf. Bruns *et al.* 2015; Papacharissi 2015). This journey began with scholarship providing initial accounts of new social media practices (Hermida 2012) to developing a richer understanding of the interplay between social media, news and audiences (Nielsen and Fletcher 2018). This opened a new thread of research oriented towards understanding the ways social media and journalism intersected, alongside reflections on the assumptions, enthusiasms, and critical blind spots within such studies, all to be considered as this line of work continues to develop (Lewis and Molyneux 2018). Rather than suggest an insufficiency in the work which has been done, this has revealed that within the complexity of digital journalism there remains much to be learned as the texture of change continues to develop. Among the emerging questions, currently being addressed, for example, is how to account for actors and audiences engaging in "dark participation" (Quandt 2018), and sharing news on "dark social" networks (Swart, Peters, and Broersma 2018).

Such critical reflection is not so much a note on the ebb and flow of meaningful studies and what they attend to, though this is only natural. Rather, it introduces to this discussion an example of how the body of work around digital journalism is coming into its own, with—as Delli Carpini (2017) has written—space for disagreements and, from them, richer developments. Thus, we can see where research has continued to reveal and then open new approaches for understanding what the audience for digital journalism may be; whether re-engaging questions of how journalists and audiences collaborate in different stages of the news production process using digital tools (Kligler-Vilenchik and Tenenboim 2019), or re-assessing the behaviours we associate with audiences and news (Groot-Kormelink 2015), or asking how journalists define their roles in relation to these audiences (Hanusch and Banjac 2019), now in a digital age. This burgeoning research agenda, and the way it continues to morph, has led to constant calls for scholars to grapple with our own position within fields of society, particularly as navigating these changes becomes all the more complex (Delli Carpini 2017). For ourselves, looking over a research field taking shape, it prompts further questions as to how to map digital journalism studies.

Beyond these approaches—which still place at their core an understanding of journalism within digital environments—work has broken from the traditional tripartite focus of content, producer, and audience to consider digital journalism within a much wider ecology. Open data platforms avail us of new avenues for telling stories of environmental degradation which draw on resources beyond journalistic endeavor (Salovaara 2016), while critical questions are posed as to what all this digital technology means for the rather non-digital environment we live in, highlighting the implications for the natural world as natural resources are consumed in order to enable the expanse of digital technologies (Miller 2015). As the material traces of journalism are increasingly hard to pin down in a digital environment which we increasingly are immersed in, and experience our worlds through (Deuze 2012), the relationship between digital news and audiences is nevertheless being reconfigured (Broersma 2019). In melding, rather than adjoining, the digital and journalism, we are further prompted to ask how we might reimagine the public, both offline and online (Wenzel 2018; Zamith and Lewis 2014)? Are end-users the new imagined audiences (Picone 2016), where the functions of media become interlaced with other technologies and platforms, including those beyond journalism's control (Ekström and Westlund 2019)?

While a further discussion of the exhaustive set of topics is implausible here, we arrive at a point where we can confidently surmise that digital journalism represents a domain of research which progressed quickly from curiosity to description, and from description towards theoretical understanding (Eldridge and Franklin 2019: 8–9). Indeed, while Witschge et al. (2016) are right to point out that ambiguity and uncertainty seem to be ever-present in the field, we are heartened that scholars have done well to keep apace in their abilities to address ambiguity and resolve uncertainty. As they have done so, we have witnessed two fields of indistinct boundaries emerge.

The first of these is a field of digital journalism. The increasingly porous (or seemingly so) boundaries of the journalistic field (Carlson and Lewis 2015; Eldridge 2018) have both absorbed and challenged new entrants to the field, including those from well beyond the newsroom (Baack 2018). The second, is the emergent field of research in Digital Journalism Studies, which has broken in part from (while remaining indebted to) the predicate field of Journalism Studies (Carlson et al. 2018).

The emergence of these two fields has also led to an opening of doors into new ways of assessing journalism beyond the cognate disciplines of politics, sociology, economy, and communication science. This has allowed digital journalism scholars to find compatriots in the fields of computer science, who help us make sense of immersive technologies (Greussing and Boomgaarden 2018; Kang et al. 2018; Kuiken et al. 2017), massive analyses of information flows (Günther, Buhl, and Quandt 2019), and developing news stories (Zamith 2019). This has introduced new methods for scholars to grab billions of pieces of content (Malik and Pfeffer 2016), as well as avenues for enriching our assessment of content using natural language processing and machine learning (Boumans and Trilling 2016), and approaches for revisiting the distance between humans and machine using Human–Machine Communication (HMC) frameworks to understand machines as not only mediators, but communicators (Lewis, Guzman, and Schmidt 2019).

As we now turn to the conceptual arguments introduced in this special issue, it is worth returning, however briefly, to what remains constant in both digital journalism and our precursor understanding of journalism and the decades of research which unpacked its meaningfulness for our everyday societies. We see in both Journalism

Studies, and in the future of Digital Journalism Studies, an opportunity for dialogue between established theories and new developments; dialogues which, if allowed to develop more fully, can imagine each of these fields anew. In doing so, we confront the challenges which face any field moving stridently towards new territory—in what directions are the boundaries expanding, and what should they nevertheless exclude? Where does Digital Journalism Studies fit within the broader range of communications research which is committed to making sense of journalism? This forces us to examine whether, for all the potential that innovative and interdisciplinary research brings, there is also risk in opening up a field of academic understanding, replete with familiar concepts, terminology, and ways of meaning making, to new types of inquiry and methods for carrying these out.

Synthesizing *Digital Journalism* (Part II)

This issue of *Digital Journalism* has sought to further advance the debate and understanding of digital journalism, and has offered us a specific opportunity to engage with the questions surrounding these two fields to further our understanding and definition of both digital journalism and Digital Journalism Studies. In order to advance this, we offer some reflexive insight into the types of articles that this very journal has published from its inception in 2013 until mid-2018 (Steensen *et al.* 2019). This research reveals a strong emphasis on the changing nature of digital platforms and a dominant social science perspective, at the expense of articles that explore, for example, history and context or which would build new and novel theories drawing on interdisciplinary knowledge. Steensen *et al.* (2019) also highlight that current definitions of digital journalism—when based on this literature—need to further consider the types of knowledge that digital journalism creates, its role as a meaning-making system, and its relationship to other social institutions and issues of power. This brings us to the second debut within this issue: the rich and diverse array of conceptual articles, each focusing on digital journalism as a key concept. These have presented us with a broad set of approaches, arguments, and authoritative definitions. In Table 1 we capture the way these authors and their contributions, both from a review of the literature and their own conceptualizations, bring such conceptual definitions into a discussion.

Looking at the table above, it is immediately apparent the field benefits from a diverse set of perspectives into how we can understand and define digital journalism. Some definitions privilege *Journalism* over *Digital* focusing on how digital technologies transform journalistic processes, practices, and norms. Steensen and colleagues have highlighted how digital journalism refers, for instance, to "transforming" journalistic processes, whereas Robinson and colleagues refer to the digital as transcendental to these processes, and Waisbord argues that the digital expands journalism. At the other end, others place *Digital* at the core of their definitions, focusing on digitization as a process running across social domains, of which journalism is but one. Duffy and Ang, for example, focus on how digitization brings its own processes, norms, and rules into journalism. While each provides its own take on digital journalism, a common thread promptly emerges in this collection of work—that referring to the "digital" is more

Table 1. Definitions of *Digital Journalism (Studies)*.

Steen Steensen, Anna M. Grøndahl Larsen, Yngve Benestad Hågvar and Birgitte Kjos Fonn, 2019, 338
Digital journalism is the transforming social practice of selecting, interpreting, editing and distributing factual information of perceived public interest to various kinds of audiences in specific, but changing genres and formats. As such, digital journalism both shapes and is shaped by new technologies and platforms, and it is marked by an increasingly symbiotic relationship with the audiences. The actors engaged in this social practice are bound by the structures of social institutions publicly recognized as journalistic institutions

Sue Robinson, Seth C. Lewis and Matt Carlson, 2019, 369–370	Andrew Duffy and Ang Peng Hwa, 2019, 382	Silvio Waisbord, 2019, 352	Jean Burgess and Edward Hurcombe, 2019, 360	Barbie Zelizer, 2019, 349
Research that involves newswork employing digital technologies in some manner, such as news websites, social platforms, mobile devices, data analytics, algorithms, etc;. Research that acknowledges how digital dynamics of journalism interact with and alter formerly discrete boundaries … and the authority and forces that go along with these changes and configurations; Research that interrogates the resulting practical and cultural transformations occurring around news and other acts of journalism as they relate to broader issues …	Digital journalism as the way in which journalism embodies the philosophies, norms, practices, values and attitudes of digitisation as they relate to society. These include the efficiency of control, storage, retrieval, accessibility and transmission of data; inclusivity, interactivity and collaboration in the propagation of information and opinion; flexibility and innovation in presenting news stories; and state, institutional and individual ownership of data and its implications for privacy and transparency	Digital journalism is the networked production, distribution and consumption of news and information. It is characterized by network settings and practices that expand the opportunities and spaces for news	Those practices of newsgathering, reporting, textual production and ancillary communication that reflect, respond to, and shape the social, cultural and economic logics of the constantly changing digital media environment. To study digital journalism is to study the transformative and isomorphic impacts of digital media technologies and business models on the practice, product and business of journalism, as well as the ways that journalistic discourses, practices and logics in turn shape the cultures and technologies of those digital media platforms through which journalism is practiced, and its products are shared and consumed	Digital journalism thus takes its meaning from both practice and rhetoric. Its practice as newsmaking embodies a set of expectations, practices, capabilities and limitations relative to those associated with pre-digital and non-digital forms, reflecting a difference of degree rather than kind. Its rhetoric heralds the hopes and anxieties associated with sustaining the journalistic enterprise as worthwhile. With the digital comprising the figure to journalism's ground, digital journalism constitutes the most recent of many conduits over time that have allowed us to imagine optimum links between journalism and its publics

Scott Eldridge, Kristy Hess, Edson Tandoc, and Oscar Westlund, 2019, 394.
Digital Journalism Studies should strive to be an academic field which critically explores, documents, and explains the interplay of digitization and journalism, continuity and change. *Digital Journalism Studies* should further strive to focus, conceptualize, and theorize tensions, configurations, power imbalances, and the debates these continue to raise for digital journalism and its futures.

than an allusion to new tools and hardware in online spaces and instead it must always be situated within a larger socio-technical environment; there, it is seated amongst broader concerns of economics, labor, organizational cultures, technological innovation and cultural and social practices. Where technology is prominent, it is also embedded within a broader set of dynamics.

We can draw further on these threads in bringing together the disparate approaches to understanding digital journalism to assess where differences are strengths which can be woven into a shared agenda within Digital Journalism Studies, one which substantiates this growing body of work into a discrete academic field. Drawing on these definitions, we turn now to developing the key ideas and provocations that our invited scholars prompt from their theoretical, geographic, and practical perspectives on digital journalism, to offer our ambitions for Digital Journalism Studies, and for this journal committed to shepherding research within the field.

For us to label such a body of work as reflective of a field is a conscious and deliberate choice to provide some necessary clarity within Digital Journalism Studies. In the growing pains of Digital Journalism Studies, questions as to whether this badge better describes a subfield of Journalism Studies writ large, or its own unique field, have continued to bubble up. This is, in a sense, reflective of the definitional struggles all societal fields experience as they seek to resolve a dominant vision which can center their priorities, and in that sense Digital Journalism Studies is not so unique. It is furthermore a reflection of the myriad approaches to understanding digital journalism as an object of study; approaches embedded in the conceptual approaches in this very issue. Yet it also reflects a group of scholars, and a body of research, well-equipped to make apparent these tensions, and in doing so to provide a vantage point towards mapping the field. As readily as scholars examine the shifting boundaries of journalism, work prodding the boundaries, the dominant visions, and the agreed sense of belonging which define Digital Journalism Studies can also be addressed. Here, struggles revolve around how best to acknowledge the antecedent legacy of Journalism Studies, while focusing attention on an increasingly distinct sphere of research focused on digital journalism.

Thus, we argue, to position Digital Journalism Studies as a sub-field of Journalism Studies, rather than an emergent field in its own right, limits its value and potential to scholarship not just within media studies and communication, but its wider interdisciplinary reach. It also continues to reinforce a journalism-centric approach when we need to consider the interplay between news, digitization, and the wider social spaces where everyday audiences and media users generate engagement with matters of public interest and the world(s) around them. As new and hybrid practices and organizations emerge, it must be argued that change occurs not just through transformation of existing and established organizations, but also in the founding of new and hybrid organizations that develop their own distinct sets of norms and values. That a bevy of introspective studies, questions, methods, and frameworks have emerged to ask key questions of digital journalism bolsters our view that this is not an area of scholarship nestled within Journalism Studies, but a field with its own core demands and replete with ways of approaching these, including those that have grown out of the work in Journalism Studies.

There is nevertheless a tension in this decision, one which also sits between the ways scholars take on digital journalism as an object of inquiry; this is, we argue, a fruitful tension, within a field which needs to have work that strives towards resolving such strains. Yet we do not, in defining a field, need to resolve this first in order to then proceed. Indeed, just as decades of journalism scholarship left open the question of "what is journalism?" to periodically be explored anew as new understandings emerged and new generations of scholars introduced new perspectives, so too do we see the tensions within Digital Journalism Studies at the core of questions which drive the field. For a field which sees its object of study—digital journalism—defined in part by its technological shifts, and in part by its journalistic legacy, the push and pull between an emphasis on *continuity* and *change*, or between *digital* and *journalism*, provides a useful way for scholars to consider their work as they grapple with discrete aspects of digital journalism. It also prompts awareness of other forces at play in the field which surrounds them. At the center of innovative work which moves from defining towards understanding, and from identifying towards theorizing, these tensions can be useful—if taken advantage of.

Digital journalism studies, and the DJS Compass (part III)

We turn now to offer a more precise forward-looking definition of the field, through which we can navigate our discussions. In the definition, below, we highlight where Digital Journalism Studies has emerged as a field, and where we as the *Digital Journalism* editorial team argue it should continue to address the mechanisms, processes, rules, philosophies and norms in seeking to make sense of digital journalism.

> **Digital Journalism Studies** should strive to be an academic field which critically explores, documents, and explains the interplay of digitization and journalism, continuity and change. Digital Journalism Studies should further strive to focus, conceptualize, and theorize tensions, configurations, power imbalances, and the debates these continue to raise for digital journalism and its futures.

Thus, the field is a place for work focused on what has changed and what remains the same, emphasizing "digitization" or "journalism", within a robust body of scholarship which continues to develop its modes of understanding while drawing on its cognate, and multiple, disciplinary backgrounds. This definition also reflects, as we have shown in Part I, the constant negotiation and renegotiation of understanding, as work moves from describing towards explaining digital journalism. While we are not alone in defining this field, we are keen to emphasize here our definition is normative. While it builds on the burgeoning line of research at its foundation, and reflective of how this has contributed to defining the field, it is equally aspirational in setting out the future ambitions for what the field should endeavor towards. In pursuit of this ambition, we metaphorically navigate between four foci which continue to shape the work ourselves and our colleagues take on.

The Digital Journalism Studies Compass

Turning now to explore the DJS Compass, we present in this section ways in which we can navigate these developments through the heuristic device of a compass, orienting between four key aspects of Digital Journalism Studies. In our metaphorical compass, Digital Journalism Studies research can be seen in relation to four key components that serve as anchor points for positioning research within the field: *digital*, *journalism*, *continuity* and *change*. As anchor points, these are relational rather than hierarchical, offering guides rather than dependent paths. In such a field, regardless of the directions one heads, a compass allows us to orient our work and the direction we are headed in, doing so in relation to the rest of the field. Just as North is made distinct in that it differs from South, East, and West, the directions of digital, journalism, continuity, and change are also made more salient in relation to one another.

Such a tool allows us to think through while remaining aware of the positionality of our work as it relates to the field around us. In reflecting on the field, and the work underpinning it, we find that such positioning is critical. We also find, as outlined in Part I, that this is often reflected in work which demonstrates an awareness of the larger body of scholarship. We consider such positioning integral in work which will continue to be developed, and yet to emerge. The DJS Compass allows us a series of ways to explore, among more general research questions, how the "digital" can, and does, help preserve a powerful position for "journalism" in society. In another direction, it helps us consider the role of journalism in generating new digital processes, practices and nodes of power. Further embedded in our imagining of such a compass, we see where it may encourage scholars to engage multiple dimensions at one time, balancing the key considerations in any one study across the other dimensions which define the field. For example, it can challenge us to consider what remains the same, and where there is "continuity" within and between digital and journalism undergoing "change".

Between "digital" and "journalism"

Moving further, and building on the conceptual essays and review essay in this issue, we have identified these dimensions as a series of, on the one hand tensions, and on the other hand opportunities. For one, such anchor points provoke debates over whether one or the other should be prioritized, thereby setting some form of "true north" for Digital Journalism Studies. Alternatively they can be viewed equally, and as

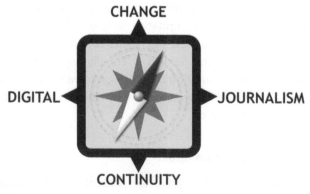

Figure 1. The DJS Compass.

such each can anchor research which charts new directions for the field. As an editorial team, this has been a salient question as we seek to steer the direction of this journal, while remaining mindful of the breadth of work around us, and that which we have yet to discover. Some scholars, for example, will continue to orient their research towards understanding and advancing journalism practice, and indeed many studies that place themselves within Digital Journalism Studies have focused on how journalism is reshaped, or for some transformed, by digitization. Burgess and Hurcombe (2019) argue as much in their contribution within this issue, highlighting the ways digitization has had an impact on news gathering processes. This is further reflected in the definitions provided by Steensen et al. (2019) from an extensive review of the literature, and in the conceptual definition proposed by Robinson, Lewis, and Carlson (2019). Their definitions point towards work which has documented how various stages of news production, for example, have been affected by digitization, and how new technologies, data, and analytics have brought about changes in both news routines as well as in how journalists conceive of their audiences (Linden 2017). Offline, scholars are focused on the ways the political economy of journalism, and the implications of decisions made in boardrooms, and shaping policy and regulation for journalism, also remain pressing concerns (Cohen 2016; Pickard 2019).

There is also, however, a growing contingent who argue the need to position the digital as central to digital journalism studies, as Duffy and Peng Hwa (2019) do in their conceptual essay, arguing that it warrants equal footing in our re-orienteering of the field. Rarely, for example, have scholars examined how journalism has *also* impacted digitization. Facebook refers to the space where a user gets to see posts from her network as the "newsfeed," clearly a reference to news platforms as socially important and recognized spaces. "Fake news" producers build networks of fake sites populated by a combination of human troll armies and bots, but ultimately designed to mimic the news ecosystem, comprising of competing news outlets pushing out often similar content—a seeming recognition of the social resonance news and journalism continues to hold. In situating digitization and journalism within the quadrants of the DJS Compass, it is important to consider that an often assumed but under explored dimension of our metaphorical instrument is that of a wider social space.

This reminds us that not only are the four directions on the compass relational, so too are the ways we conceive of their importance at a larger scale. At the base of our compass, we position the domains of everyday life and the spaces and places in which people interact—what we argue should serve as the common denominator between journalism and the digital moving forward. In this way, the process of digitization serves as an exemplar of the interplay between the digital and the journalism—that is, the way domains of social life are structured and restructured around digital communication and media infrastructures. And further, even as our attention shifts online and we make sense of the digital ecosystem as a location for journalism, and its audiences, the spaces and places where news is created or engaged with continue to have purchase, even when they seem destined to be linked to the screens we view content through (Gutsche and Hess 2018; Peters 2012). So too do the communities within which digital journalism is found (Bosch 2014), and the ways in which we navigate towards, and through, these spaces.

Between "continuity" and "change"

As a second set of guiding points, the continuum between *continuity* and *change* forms a red thread throughout many of the existing approaches to, and discussions of, digital journalism. More generally, over the past decade journalism has been surrounded by a discourse giving emphasis to crisis. Many of those come from researchers, practitioners and pundits alike who have made calls for the need to innovate, innovate, and innovate more. Essentially, these have been calls for change, jumping on the bandwagon, appropriating, and developing emerging technologies of diverse kinds for journalism's purposes. Critically, Zelizer (2019) in her essay in this issue reminds us that we can draw meaning from such discussions, as digital journalism is defined both by the practices involved *and* the rhetoric surrounding these. Discourse around change has tended to evolve from viewing change as a revolution to change as deconstruction, in the sense that Digital Journalism Studies today is preoccupied with deconstructing previously established notions of what journalism is (Steensen and Ahva 2015). If we take one step back and reflect on these normative calls for change, as Zelizer encourages, we can conclude that there is now, as has been the case previously (Eldridge 2015; Peters and Carlson 2018), a pro-innovation bias. Scholars have been attracted by "the bright, shiny things" (Posetti 2018), and journalists fall into reporting on emerging technology such as artificial intelligence largely in an industry-led way (Brennen, Howard, and Nielsen 2018).

This has brought about a dislocation of journalism, with news appearing on platforms which are non-proprietary to news media organizations, affecting not only audience traffic and revenue, but the very epistemic practices of news media as they adapt to producing content for digital platforms such as Facebook and Twitter (Ekström and Westlund, 2019), including by engaging in "platform counterbalancing", strategically addressing the influence of social media platforms (Chua and Westlund 2019; c.f. Newman 2019). These studies nevertheless reflect how news industries, with their isomorphic and path-dependent behaviors, often strive towards embracing emerging technologies and opportunities, bringing into starker relief the tension Lewis (2012) spoke of, as control from homespun websites shifted to social media spaces and platforms in new, complex, entanglements with news producers (Artwick 2018; Westlund and Ekström 2018). This includes examining, for instance, what journalists, technologists and businesspeople do, and how they relate to each other. Such shifts have also signaled the expansion of a journalistic field beyond the erstwhile newsroom and its traditional denizens (Lewis and Westlund 2015; Nielsen 2012; Westlund 2011; Wu, Tandoc, and Simon 2019). Recent research also includes the study of digital journalism in relation to civic technologists and Web analytics firms external to the news organizations (Baack 2018; Belair-Gagnon and Holton 2018).

In our discussion of continuity and change, therefore, we do not subscribe to any singlehanded rhetoric calling for innovation, as there may well be great reasons for not engaging in innovation as well. Moreover, the pro-innovation bias arguments in journalism have repeatedly boiled down to discussions of how the news media industries are innovating less and performing less well than other industries. However, few scholars provide any substantial basis or evidence for such comparison, and those who do report relatively minor differences, based on crude measures of money spent on innovation as reported by companies, which may not capture innovativeness (see, e.g., Bleyen, Lindmark, Ranaivoson, and Ballon 2014). Further, as Waisbord (2019) helpfully highlights here, while innovation and technologies have a place within *Digital Journalism* and Digital Journalism Studies, they are often best seen as "opportunities and spaces" for news, where scholars examine tendencies towards change, alongside the resonance of continuity. Thus, we see the engagement with emergent change as best set in relation to the ways it draws and departs from aspects of continuity to speak meaningfully about digital journalism within a more complex interrelationship.

Conclusion

There is an inherent tension in Digital Journalism Studies between the priorities placed on either "digital" or "journalism", as well as between "change" and "continuity". We recognize that the quick transformations taking place in digital journalism as an object of inquiry may also result in challenges with regards to what theoretical frameworks can be sensible to employ, and sometimes may be absent altogether. Nevertheless, we argue it can be useful to present, clarify, and employ key concepts that guide the research design and analysis, including points of departure and continuous threads. By commissioning conceptual articles in *Digital Journalism* on timely and important concepts, from key scholars working in distinct areas of research, we strive towards facilitating the advancement of the field in a way that balances such aspects of continuity and change. Importantly, we envision such conceptual articles will serve as anchoring points which, by applying these in future work, scholars can continue to contribute to continuity within the field. Mindful of the tensions and viewpoints shaping the field, the *Digital Journalism* Editorial Team will work towards careful consideration of new concepts, scrutinizing those which hold little potential for being used in empirical research or which struggle to situate themselves within the broader field.

The debates in this issue present deep divides, divisions which can be made productive and which are evident within our own editorial team and our approaches to scholarship. At the risk of overusing a very technological cliché, these divisions are a feature, not a bug. They highlight that the very work of Digital Journalism Studies is not to dismiss either side but to acknowledge these tensions, accept and/or challenge them through rigorous study, in the pursuit of generating new and hybrid ways of understanding digital journalism and its place within the world around us.

As a guide, the DJS Compass should help navigate our work in this pursuit, and a means of orienting work which conceives of digital journalism, and Digital Journalism Studies, within a broader body of work concerned with similar dynamics, mindful of that which surrounds it. Yet, as the field continues to move forward, we caution that inasmuch as it offers us a means to position ourselves, there is no "true north" in our compass. Drawing from the conceptual and review essays in this issue, and our discussion above, the five key points below provide further guidance to consider moving forward. Following these, Digital Journalism Studies research should work towards:

- Acknowledging the tension between continuity and change (i.e., avoid solely emphasizing "new" innovation without *also* embracing what has been before).

- Embracing scholarship that positions itself in relation to extant theories and concepts, including interdisciplinary perspectives that advance understandings of digital journalism. This includes work which challenges those theories which have been dominant, but may be due for reconsideration.
- Avoid confining research to familiar spaces of news production, distribution, or consumption, nor to be limited to recognizable forms of content, but instead push towards examining where to locate journalism within the digital.
- Rethinking the relationship between journalism and digitization—considering digital journalism as a discrete focus of research, and Digital Journalism Studies as a discrete domain of research.
- Embracing work which recognizes the ongoing power struggles between individuals and institutions (new and existing) in society, including those shaping or shaped by journalism, technology, and the ways this has an impact on our societies, for journalism, its publics, the individuals involved, and the worlds around us.

Guided by the DJS Compass, and considering these priorities, we see digital journalism as something that should continue to be theorized, conceptualized, and studied in a contextual and relational way that makes central this tension between the push and pull between digital technology and journalism, and between what has changed with digital journalism and what it owes to its journalistic forebears.

For this journal, our ambitious and straightforward *vision* reflects these priorities, and remains focused on fostering such discussions: *Digital Journalism* should be the most important journal in the world for research in Digital Journalism Studies. By this we mean that the journal should feature a substantial volume of high-quality research into digital journalism, making it the primary gateway to access such work. Moreover, the importance of the research published is demonstrated in terms of the level of depth and insight which can be found in the work we publish, and may be further demonstrated by how widely the articles are being downloaded and read (by scholars, students, and practitioners), and to what extent the articles are cited in other scientific publications. This means that, qualitatively, we strive towards publishing articles which advance the field by further developing and supporting existing theories and concepts, or presenting empirical evidence that questions these foundations.

As we look forward, we also see *Digital Journalism* as a space for scholars positing new concepts and theories that importantly acknowledge or pose a challenge to other traditional approaches or contemporary ideas and can be put to use in digital journalism practice. We firmly believe that the research published in *Digital Journalism* should balance continuity and change; continuity in terms of taking departure in theoretical frameworks and/or conceptual constructs, and change in terms of continuously identifying and studying important areas of change. The importance of research can also be seen in terms of public engagement, gaining significance among media managers, journalists and policy makers, especially when such stakeholders reconfigure their practices or policy based on research published. We hope our compass helps navigate the path towards fulfilling our ultimate aim:

> That *Digital Journalism* should serve as an authoritative and forerunning journal advancing the field of digital journalism studies, by publishing double-blind peer-

reviewed articles that make theoretical and/or conceptual advancements, as well as those which offer critical and reflexive scholarly discussions and where, in all empirical work published, scholars must apply sound methods and carry out rigorous analysis. *Digital Journalism* further aims to identify and engage with submissions that truly engage with the dynamic, interwoven, and interrelated aspects of digital journalism, its various concepts and definitions, and the growth of Digital Journalism Studies as a field benefiting from such work.

Acknowledgments

We thank Gaute Heggen at Oslo Metropolitan University for helping us create the DJS Compass and Table of definitions. We are also grateful to the contributors in this issue for providing the conceptual definitions and research review which we engage with here, as well as the anonymous peer reviewers and colleagues who supported their development. Our thanks go as well to Sue Robinson and Stefan Baack who offered feedback on our own endeavor in this article and whose comments helped us add further clarity to our argument. Finally, our thanks extend to Bob Franklin for setting us on this intellectual course.

ORCID

Scott A. Eldridge http://orcid.org/0000-0002-2184-1509
Kristy Hess http://orcid.org/0000-0003-3027-7492
Edson C. Tandoc http://orcid.org/0000-0002-8740-9313
Oscar Westlund http://orcid.org/0000-0002-2533-6737

References

Allan, Stuart. 2006. *Online News: Journalism and the Internet*. Maidenhead: Open University Press.
Artwick, Claudette. 2018. *Social Media Livestreaming: Design for Disruption?* Abingdon: Routledge.
Baack, Stefan. 2018. "Practically Engaged: The Entanglements Between Data Journalism and Civic Tech." *Digital Journalism* 6 (6): 673–692.
Belair-Gagnon, Valerie, and Avery Holton. 2018. "Boundary Work, Interloper Media, and Analytics in Newsrooms: An Analysis of the Roles of Web Analytics Companies in News Production." *Digital Journalism* 6 (4): 492–508.
Bleyen, Valérie-Anne; Sven Lindmark, Heritiana Ranaivoson, and Pieter Ballon. 2014. "A Typology of Media Innovations: Insights from An Exploratory Study." *Journal of Media Innovations*, 1 (1): 28–51.
Brennen, Scott, Philip N. Howard, and Rasmus Kleis Nielsen. 2018. *An Industry-Led Debate: How UK Media Cover Artificial Intelligence*, RISJ Fact-Sheet. Oxford: University of Oxford.
Boczkowski, Pablo. 2004. "The Processes of Adopting Multimedia and Interactivity in Three Online Newsrooms." *Journal of Communication* 54 (2): 197–213.
Boczkowski, Pablo, and C. W. Anderson. 2018. *Remaking the News*. Cambridge: MIT Press.
Bosch, Tanja. 2014. "Social Media and Community Radio Journalism in South Africa." *Digital Journalism* 2 (1): 29–43.
Boumans, Jelle W., and Damian Trilling. 2016. "Taking Stock of the Toolkit: An Overview of Relevant Automated Content Analysis Approaches and Techniques for Digital Journalism." *Digital Journalism* 4 (1): 8–23.
Braun, Joshua A., and Jessica L. Eklund. 2019. "Fake News, Real Money: Ad Tech Platforms, Profit-Driven Hoaxes, and the Business of Journalism," *Digital Journalism* 7 (1): 1–21.

Broersma, Marcel. 2019. "Epilogue: Situating Journalism in the Digital: A Plea For Studying News Flows, Users, and Materiality." In *The Routledge Handbook of Developments in Digital Journalism Studies*, edited by Scott Eldridge and Bob Franklin, 515–526. Abingdon: Routledge.

Bruns, Axel. 2005. *Gatewatching: Collaborative Online News Production*. Oxford: Peter Lang.

Bruns, Axel, Gunn Enli, Eli Skogerbo, Anders Olof Larsson, and Christian Christensen. 2015. *The Routledge Companion to Social Media and Politics*. Abingdon: Routledge.

Burgess, Jean, and Edward Hurcombe. 2019. "Digital Journalism as Symptom, Response, and Agent of Change," *Digital Journalism* 7 (3): 359–367.

Caplan, Robyn, and Danah Boyd. 2018. Isomorphism Through Algorithms: Institutional Dependencies in the Case of Facebook." *Big Data and Society*. https://doi.org/10.1177/2053951718757253

Carlson, Matt. 2015. "Introduction: The Many Boundaries of Journalism." In *Boundaries of Journalism*, edited by Matt Carlson and Seth C. Lewis, 1–18. Abingdon: Routledge.

Carlson, Matt, and Seth C. Lewis. 2015. *Boundaries of Journalism*. Abingdon: Routledge.

Carlson, Matt, Sue Robinson, Seth C. Lewis, and Daniel Berkowitz. 2018. "Journalism Studies and its Core Commitments: The Making of a Communication Field." *Journal of Communication* 68 (1): 6–25.

Chua, Sherwin, Oscar Westlund. 2019. "Audience-Centric Engagement, Collaboration Culture and Platform Counterbalancing: A Longitudinal Study of Ongoing Sensemaking of Emerging Technologies." *Media and Communication* 7 (1): 153–165.

Cohen, Nicole. 2016. *Writers' Rights*. Montreal: McGill-Queen's University Press.

Curran, James, Natalie Fenton, and Des Freedman. 2012. *Misunderstanding the Internet*. Abingdon: Routledge.

Delli Carpini, Michael. 2017. "Postscript: The Who, What, When, Where, Why, and How of Journalism and Journalism Studies." In *Remaking the News*, edited by Pablo J. Boczkowski, and C. W. Anderson, 273–288. Cambridge: MIT Press.

Deuze, Mark. 2005. "What is Journalism? Professional Identity and Ideology of Journalists Reconsidered." *Journalism* 6 (4): 442–464.

Deuze, Mark. 2012. *Media Life*. Cambridge: Polity.

Duffy, Andrew, and Ang Peng Hwa. 2019. "Digital Journalism: Defined, Refined, or Re-defined," *Digital Journalism* 7 (3): 378–385.

Ekström, Mats, and Oscar Westlund. 2019. "The Dislocation of News Journalism: A Conceptual Framework for the Study of Epistemologies of Digital Journalism." *Media and Communication* 7 (1): 259–270.

Eldridge, Scott. 2015. Continuity and Change: Historicizing the Emergence of Online Journalism. In *The Routledge Companion to British Media History*, edited by Martin Conboy and John Steel, 528–538. Abingdon: Routledge.

Eldridge, Scott. 2018. *Online Journalism from the Periphery: Interloper Media and the Journalistic Field*. Abingdon: Routledge.

Eldridge, Scott, and Bob Franklin. 2019. "Introducing the Complexities of Developments in Digital Journalism Studies." In *The Routledge Handbook of Developments in Digital Journalism Studies*, edited by Scott Eldridge and Bob Franklin, 1–12. Abingdon: Routledge.

Errico, Marcus. 1997. "The Evolution of the Summary News Lead." *Media History Monographs*, 1 (1).

Franklin, Bob, and Scott Eldridge. 2017. *The Routledge Companion to Digital Journalism Studies*. Abingdon: Routledge.

Greussing, Esther, and Hajo Boomgaarden. 2018. "Simply Bells and Whistles?: Cognitive Effects of Visual Aesthetics in Digital Longforms" *Digital Journalism*. 7 (2): 273–293.

Günther, Elisabeth, Florian Buhl, and Thorsten Quandt. 2019. "Reconstructing the Dynamics of the Digital News Ecosystem: A Case Study on News Diffusion Processes." In *The Routledge Handbook of Developments in Digital Journalism Studies*, edited by Scott Eldridge and Bob Franklin, 118–131. Abingdon: Routledge.

Gutsche, Robert, and Kristy Hess. 2018. *Geographies of Journalism: The Imaginative Power of Place in Digital News*. Abingdon: Routledge.

Hanusch, Folker and Banjac, Sandra. 2019. "Studying Role Conceptions in a Digital Age: A Critical Appraisal." In *The Routledge Handbook of Developments in Digital Journalism Studies*, edited by Scott Eldridge and Bob Franklin, 28–39. Abingdon: Routledge.

Hermida, Alfred. 2012. "Social Journalism: Exploring How Social Media is Shaping Journalism." In *The Handbook of Global Online Journalism*, edited by Eugenia Siapera and Andreas Veglis, 309–328. Oxford: Wiley-Blackwell.

Kang, Seok; Erin O'Brien, Arturo Villarreal, Wansoo Lee, and Chad Mahood. 2018. "Immersive Journalism and Telepresence: Does Virtual Reality News Use Affect News Credibility? *Digital Journalism*.

Karlsson, Michael, and Helle Sjøvaag. 2016. "Research Methods in an Age of Digital Journalism." *Digital Journalism* 4 (1): 1–7.

Kuiken, Jeffrey, Anne Schuth, Martijn Spitters, and Maarten Marx. 2017. "Effective Headlines of Newspaper Articles in a Digital Environment". *Digital Journalism* 5 (10): 1300–1314.

Kligler-Vilenchik, N., and O. Tenenboim. 2019, forthcoming. "Sustained Journalist–Audience Reciprocity in a Meso-Newspace: The Case of a Journalistic WhatsApp Group." *New Media and Society*.

Lewis, Seth C. 2012. "The Tension Between Professional Control and Open Participation: Journalism and its Boundaries" *Information, Communication and Society* 15 (6): 836–866.

Lewis, Seth C. 2019, forthcoming. "Journalism." In *The International Encyclopedia of Journalism Studies*, edited by Tim P. Vos and Folker Hanusch (General Editors), Dimitra Dimitrakopoulou, Margaretha Geertsema-Sligh and Annika Sehl (Associate Editors). New York: Wiley.

Lewis, Seth C., and Logan Molyneux. 2018. "A decade of research on social media and journalism: Assumptions, blind 598 spots, and a way forward." *Media and Communication*, 6 (4): 11–23.

Lewis, Seth. C., Andrea. L. Guzman, and Thomas R. Schmidt. 2019. "Automation, Journalism, and Human-Machine Communication: Rethinking Roles and Relationships of Humans and Machines in News." *Digital Journalism*, https://doi.org/10.1080/21670811.2019.1577147.

Lewis, Seth, and Oscar Westlund. 2015. "Actors, Actants, Audiences, and Activities in Cross-Media News Work: A Matrix and a Research Agenda." *Digital Journalism* 3 (1): 19–37.

Linden, Carl-Gustav. 2017. "Decades of Automation in the Newsroom: Why Are There Still So Many Jobs in Journalism?" *Digital Journalism* 5 (2): 123–140.

Malik, Momin, and Jürgen Pfeffer. 2016. "A Macroscopic Analysis of News Content in Twitter." *Digital Journalism* 4 (8): 955–979.

Miller, Toby. 2015. "Unsustainable Journalism." *Digital Journalism* 3 (5): 653–663.

Myllylahti, Merja. 2018. "An Attention Economy Trap? An Empirical Investigation into Four News Companies' Facebook Traffic and Social Media Revenue." *Journal of Media Business Studies*.

Newman, Nic. 2019. *Journalism, Media and Technology Trends and Predictions 2019, Digital News Project 2019*. Oxford: RISJ, University of Oxford.

Nielsen, Rasmus Kleis. 2012. "How Newspapers Began to Blog: Recognizing the Role of Technologists in Old Media Organizations' Development of New Media Technologies." *Information, Communication and Society* 15 (6): 959–978.

Nielsen, Rasmus Kleis, and Richard Fletcher. 2018. "Are People Incidentally Exposed to News On Social Media? A Comparative Analysis." *New Media and Society* 20 (7): 2450–2468.

Papacharissi, Zizi. 2015. "Toward New Journalism(s)." *Journalism Studies* 16 (1): 27–40.

Peters, Chris. 2012. "Journalism to GO: The Changing Spaces of News Consumption." *Journalism Studies* 13 (5–6): 695–705.

Peters, Chris, and Marcel Broersma. 2013. *Rethinking Journalism*. Abingdon: Routledge.

Peters, Chris, and Matt Carlson. 2018. "Conceptualizing Change in Journalism Studies: Why Change At All?" *Journalism*.

Pickard, Victor. 2019. "Digital Journalism and Regulation: Ownership and control." In *The Routledge Handbook of Developments in Digital Journalism Studies*, edited by Scott Eldridge and Bob Franklin. 211–222. Abingdon: Routledge.

Picone, Ike. 2016. "Grasping the Digital News User: Conceptual and Methodological Advances in News Use Studies." *Digital Journalism* 4 (1): 125–141.

Posetti, Julie. 2018. *Time to Step Away from the 'Bright, Shiny Things'? Towards a Sustainable Model of Journalism Innovation in an Era of Perpetual Change. RISJ Research Report*. Oxford: University of Oxford.

Quandt, Thorsten. 2018. "Dark Participation." *Media and Communication* 6 (4): 36–48.

Robinson, Sue, Seth C. Lewis, and Matt Carlson. 2019. "Locating the 'Digital' in Journalism Studies: Transformations in Research." *Digital Journalism* 7 (3): 368–377.

Robinson, Sue. 2006. "The Mission of the J-Blog: Recapturing Journalistic Authority Online." *Journalism* 7 (1): 65–83.

Rosen, Jay. 2006. "The People Formerly Known as the Audience." *Huffington Post*. https://www.huffingtonpost.com/jay-rosen/the-people-formerly-known_1_b_24113.html

Salovaara, Inka. 2016. "Participatory Maps: Digital Cartographies and the New Ecology of Journalism." *Digital Journalism* 4 (7): 827–837.

Singer, Jane. 2003. "Who Are These Guys?: The Online Challenge to the Notion of Journalistic Professionalism." *Journalism* 4 (2): 139–163.

Steensen, Steen, and Laura Ahva. 2015. "Theories of Journalism in a Digital age: An Exploration and Introduction." *Digital Journalism* 3 (1): 1–18.

Steensen Steen, Anna M. Larsen, Yngve Hågvar, and Birgitte Fonn. 2019. "What Does Digital Journalism Studies Look Like?" *Digital Journalism* 7 (3): 320–342.

Swart, Joelle, Chris Peters, and Marcel Broersma. 2018. "Shedding Light on the Dark Social: The Connective Role of News and Journalism in Social Media Communities." *New Media and Society* 20 (11): 4329–4345.

Tandoc, Edson, Rich Ling, and Zheng Wei Lim. 2018. "Defining 'Fake News': A Typology of Scholarly Definitions." *Digital Journalism* 6 (2): 137–153.

Tandoc, Edson, Rich Ling, Oscar Westlund, Andrew Duffy, Debbie Goh, Zheng Wei Lim. 2018. "Audiences' Acts of Authentication: A Conceptual Framework." *New Media and Society* 20 (4): 2745–2763.

Waisbord, Silvio. 2019. "The 5Ws and 1H of Digital Journalism." *Digital Journalism* 7 (3): 351–358.

Waisbord, Silvio. 2018. "Truth is What Happens to News: On Journalism, Fake News, and Post-Truth." *Journalism Studies* 19 (13): 1866–1878.

Wenzel, Andrea. 2018. "Red State, Purple Town: Polarized Communities and Local Journalism In Rural and Small-Town Kentucky." *Journalism*.

Westlund, Oscar. 2011. *Cross-media News Work—Sensemaking of the Mobile Media (R)evolution*, JMG Book Series No. 64. Gothenburg: University of Gothenburg. https://gupea.ub.gu.se/bitstream/2077/28118/1/gupea_2077_28118_1.pdf.

Westlund, Oscar, and Mats Ekström. 2018. "News and Participation through and beyond Proprietary Platforms in an Age of Social Media." *Media and Communication* 6 (4): 1–10.

Westlund, Oscar, and Seth C. Lewis. 2016. "Mapping the Human–Machine Divide in Journalism". In *The Sage Handbook of Digital Journalism*, edited by Witschge, Tamara, C. W. Anderson, David Domingo, and Alfred Hermida, 341–353. London: Sage.

Witschge, Tamara, C. W. Anderson, David Domingo, and Alfred Hermida. 2016. *The Sage Handbook of Digital Journalism*. London: Sage.

Wu, Shangyuan, Edson Tandoc, and Charles Salmon. 2019. "When Journalism and Automation Intersect: Assessing the Influence of the Technological Field on Contemporary Newsrooms." *Journalism Practice*.

Zamith, Rodrigo. 2019. "Innovation in Content Analysis: Freezing the Flow of Liquid News." In *The Routledge Handbook of Developments in Digital Journalism Studies*, edited by Scott Eldridge and Bob Franklin, 93–104. Abingdon: Routledge.

Zamith, Rodrigo, and Seth C. Lewis. 2014. "From Public Spaces to Public Sphere: Rethinking Systems for Reader Comments on Online News Sites" *Digital Journalism* 2 (4): 558–574.

Zelizer, Barbie. 2019. Why Journalism is About More Than Digital Technology," *Digital Journalism* 7 (3): 343–350.

Index